"Leading an organization is all about guiding people toward a vision. You should have daily conversations with your team and stakeholders about where things are and where they need to be. This book is foundational for these key conversations, which are essential to business and raising team performance. I was fortunate enough to work with Jen early in my career and have continued to call on her expertise during my career transitions. I highly recommend this book for anyone who manages people."

—**Karrie Trauth,** *former director and program manager, Northrop Grumman Ship Systems; current senior vice president, Shell Shipping & Maritime*

"I was initially skeptical to work with an executive coach, imagining someone who spoke in corporate jargon and who wasn't relatable. From the moment Jen walked into my office wearing skull boots, my concerns vanished! She is easy to talk with and has an innate ability to quickly and effectively help identify common and not-so-common barriers that leaders face. She has been a wonderful sounding board and has always provided authentic and practical insights that have helped me grow in my career and in life. This book is an outstanding extension of her coaching expertise."

—**Jennifer Dunn,** *communications executive, protocol and special events leader*

Ron –
Thank you for being the first at NNS to fully support this work!
Thank you for choosing me as your coach! Your confidence, trust and friendship continues to be invaluable to me.

Jen

Praise for *Own Up!*

"Leading a large, national organization that is very ᵣ dependent upon the performance of its people is a challᵉ let alone trying to transform behaviors to shift the cultᵤ the organization. Having a common approach and langᵍ to managing performance and holding people accounᵗ to desired behaviors and outcomes is critical to success. book is an essential primer for doing just that."

—**John Mulcahy,** *chairman, Mirvac Group; former ₛ executive, Commonwealth Bank Australia; and CEO, Suᵣ*

"I've worked in the past with Jen Long as an executive ᵈ both to my myself and to leaders in the organizations ᵂ which I have worked. She was quick to impress with a uᵣ ability to call any manager or executive at any level on own bullsh*t in an eye-opening way to create a unique of self-awareness and internal desire, and commitmeₙ change. Reading her book is no different than the couᵣ career- and organization-changing conversations I've with Jen. The call to change, improve, be better, and one's self and one's team accountable is strong and crieₛ delightfully loud in Jen's own terrifically impactful and mendously inspiring voice."

—**Josh LeFebvre,** *director of learning and developᵣ RSM Consulting*

"Jen provides a thoughtful approach to leadership that combines accountability with respectfulness and innovative strategies with time-trusted tactics. She's helped me to be more self-aware and challenged me to think of every interaction as an opportunity to grow and learn."

—**Jennifer Boykin,** *defense executive, US Merchant Marine Academy alumnus and board member, STEM advocate*

Jennifer T. Long

How To Hold People
Accountable
Without All The Drama

ForbesBooks

Published by ForbesBooks, Charleston, South Carolina.
Member of Advantage Media Group.

ForbesBooks is a registered trademark, and the ForbesBooks colophon is a trademark of Forbes Media, LLC.

Printed in the United States of America.

10 9 8 7 6 5 4 3 2 1

ISBN: 978-1-95588-407-5
LCCN: 2021918802

Cover design and Illustrations by Angie Lee, Grindstone Graphics, Inc.
Photography by Mark G. Lewis.

This custom publication is intended to provide accurate information and the opinions of the author in regard to the subject matter covered. It is sold with the understanding that the publisher, Advantage|ForbesBooks, is not engaged in rendering legal, financial, or professional services of any kind. If legal advice or other expert assistance is required, the reader is advised to seek the services of a competent professional.

Advantage Media Group is proud to be a part of the Tree Neutral® program. Tree Neutral offsets the number of trees consumed in the production and printing of this book by taking proactive steps such as planting trees in direct proportion to the number of trees used to print books. To learn more about Tree Neutral, please visit **www.treeneutral.com**.

Since 1917, Forbes has remained steadfast in its mission to serve as the defining voice of entrepreneurial capitalism. ForbesBooks, launched in 2016 through a partnership with Advantage Media Group, furthers that aim by helping business and thought leaders bring their stories, passion, and knowledge to the forefront in custom books. Opinions expressed by ForbesBooks authors are their own. To be considered for publication, please visit **www.forbesbooks.com**.

This book is dedicated to my mother, Dr. Cynthia S. Thero—my mentor, my colleague, my partner in crime. Forever the teacher and coach, her lessons continue to be invaluable. She is the foundation of all that is here in this book.

CONTENTS

PART III: TIME SHIFT

Your Conversations *Are* Your Relationships

WHENEVER AND WHEREVER people work together for any reason, accountability is either a stated or assumed part of *the deal*, a tenet of the job, and the basis of any genuinely mutual agreement. Some of us do it well, and some of us don't; however, we can all do better. Getting accountability right in the workplace continues to be a challenge across the globe and in organizations large, medium, and small. Conversations about accountability are pivotal conversations that can change everything. They can change results. They can change relationships. They can change culture.

Many people today are looking for a rehumanized and more humane work experience. That demand is reflected in the changing titles organizations are using to name and redefine traditional human resource roles. *People* management is replacing *talent* management. In human resources departments, we see titles like VP of People or Manager of Employee Insights. Along with changes in titles and job descriptions, traditional performance reviews and management processes are getting tossed aside. There's an increased need for interpersonal skills to be leveraged strategically in order for companies to stay competitive in business.

It's as if all the technology tools, platforms, apps, robots, artificial intelligence, and machine learning we have at our disposal have only made us more aware that we don't succeed alone. Our work is something we share in common—with our teams, colleagues, direct reports, leaders, partners, and still others. In other words, our human connections are critical, even more so as we realize that much of our success in business is based on human capital; for some businesses, people are the sole differentiator.

Given workforce demographics and the growing economic demand that businesses emphasize attracting, developing, and retaining talent, managing and leading people have never been more challenging. Management teams are critical because in addition to the daily work of generating business results, most of the *attracting*, *developing*, and *retaining* of talent falls to them as well. Your managers—a relatively small percentage of the people in your business—are powerful stewards of your culture. And today, the management paradigm is shifting. We are moving from a view of managers who "marshal resources, lay out plans, and spur effort" to a view of individuals who can motivate and align, coordinate, develop talent, build and nurture relationships, and effectively balance demands.[1] Additionally, their capacity to be good stewards has a unique twenty-first-century measure—called employee engagement—defined by the Gallup organization as "those who are involved in, enthusiastic about, and committed to their work and workplace" or to "going the extra mile."[2] Today, more than ever before, companies are using their organizational data to understand cultural challenges and management mindsets and to glean a stronger human capital strategy.

Accountability is repeatedly found to be an essential ingredient and a foundational driver of organizational success. Engagement in and of itself is not a strategy. It's an outcome. It's what you get when

---

1   Gary Hamel, *The Future of Management* (Harvard Business Press, 2007), 20.

2   "What Is Employee Engagement and How Do You Improve It?" Gallup, 2021, https://www.gallup.com/workplace/285674/improve-employee-engagement-workplace.aspx.

you already have accountability for performance. Engagement is what you get when management actually gets better at *doing* accountability well and consistently.

It's the same old story. A survey conducted by CareerBuilder.com back in 2011 shows that as many as 58 percent of managers have not been formally trained to lead others.[3] A Harvard Business survey showed that 69 percent of managers are uncomfortable communicating with employees, with 37 percent of those managers stating they are uncomfortable giving direct feedback.[4] These results seem like yesterday's news. Although communication is recognized as a fundamental area of capability, nearly all who perform in the role of managers and leaders struggle with one or more of the following:

- Anxiety over having a tough performance conversation

- Making incorrect assumptions about what employees know or understand about the work

- Making snap judgments about why things went wrong or why things aren't done

- Not wanting to feel awkward when communicating disappointment or frustration

- Managing conflict, especially employees who can't get along or team members with no trust in each other

- Being too nice instead of being super clear about poor performance

3 Allison Nawoj, "More Than One-Quarter of Managers Said They Weren't Ready to Lead When They Began Managing Others, Finds New CareerBuilder Survey," CareerBuilder, March 28, 2011, press release.

4 Karen Twaronite, "A Global Survey on the Ambiguous State of Employee Trust," Harvard Business Review, July 22, 2016, https://hbr.org/2016/07/a-global-survey-on-the-ambiguous-state-of-employee-trust.

- Tapping into an employee's intrinsic motivators to get them to initiate change or make improvements

- Losing patience when employees fail to take up their feedback or coaching efforts

We may not feel good about that list, but there is work we can do to address it. Not only does developing accountability skills within an organization dramatically enhance communication; doing so also develops skills in problem-solving, critical thinking, collaboration, feedback, and relationship building. And accountability skills are transferable insofar as they can be utilized across functions throughout a career. These skills are applicable at every level of management, from frontline to C-suite, and in every direction, including down-line to employees, across from peer to peer, and up-line to senior managers and leaders.

I've designed this book to directly address the very issues with which managers struggle most when it comes to implementing a clear and convincing approach to workplace accountability. I'll offer you a blueprint that takes away the guesswork around conversations that are all too often perceived to be *difficult, crucial,* and *fierce,* when in fact they are none of those things. I'll also show you how to remove the confusion and distress that typically accompany the way we understand and approach accountability and the things we end up saying—or otherwise conveying—when we attempt to address it. I well know that you can confront accountability issues without all the drama; I know, too, that once you begin practicing and developing the skills I'll outline for you here, you'll be much more comfortable with your work relationships and much more likely to see employee productivity and satisfaction rise as a result.

This book stitches together two key issues for managers seeking to drive accountability: effectively managing performance and effectively coaching and developing others. I distinguish these with good reason. There are many means to *coach* employee improvement, but study after study finds that investment in coaching is not paying off as anticipated. Managers feeling overwhelmed or underresourced, unprepared, and results-focused do not take or make the time to coach, and this is because they do not effectively hold employees accountable for their performance in the first place. If you can name it, they can own it. If they can own it, they can change it. If a manager cannot *name it*—meaning give the right feedback on the right thing—an employee cannot take ownership for their performance, and therefore they will not change that performance, rendering moot any effort to coach and develop that employee. This book offers you a framework for understanding why some communication techniques are preferable to others and a roadmap for plotting your skill-development journey so that your coaching efforts have a better chance of success.

> If you can name it, they can own it. If they can own it, they can change it.

Accountability at Work? Let's Talk about Drama.

My first love, and my first career, was directing theater. I studied theater in college and found the creative process wholly rewarding. For me, it's the ultimate collaborative, team-centered experience for creative people, besides maybe being in a band. In the theater, you learn a lot about others—quickly. You have to tune in to people's motivations and idiosyncrasies to see how you can leverage their strengths. The lessons of the theater are the lessons of working with people, of engaging in convincing dialogue, of creating desired emotional responses and outcomes.

The longer I've worked with corporate managers and leaders, the more acutely aware I've become of the ways that some big ideas from theater apply to accountability conversations.

Unexpected Results/Events

Let's start with the idea of drama itself—it's an exciting, emotional, or unexpected series of events or set of circumstances. When it comes to accountability, drama can be what happens in response to circumstances around poor performance. It can involve finger-pointing, the blame game, avoidance, denial, and a host of other high-stakes feelings and actions in which everyone gets worked up instead of being focused, calm, and reflective. In the theater, the key is to draw pleasure and enjoyment or at minimum to be moved by the characters engaged in the drama, whereas in the workplace, the key is to recognize the emotional responses for what they are instead of engaging or creating a spectacle. Habits of the theater actually offer us insight into how to *disengage* from the drama so as to be focused and reflective in your communications.

Contextual Analysis around Expectations

When you operate in terms of character and character motivation, you get really good at being able to stand outside a situation and see it through a more critical lens. You get good at taking a situation and evaluating it from multiple perspectives. This same capability gives managers the edge they need to remain outside the fray and do better performance analysis with their people. It also means they're able to question their own motivations: *Why am I responding in this manner? What do I want?* Those are questions that live right next door to "What's my expectation?"—which is *the* fundamental question when it comes to performance management and navigating accountability.

Confidence in Conversation and Interaction with People

Anyone who's ever done improv, either as an actor or for fun or even at a corporate learning event, understands the power of "yes, and" as a tool for improvisational interaction effectiveness. Resistance in conversation—having to be right or needing to prove your point—is resistance in interaction. But accepting what's been said—*yes, and*—is the easiest and fastest way to remain in a discovery phase and get closer to agreement or resolution. While it's used as a story-building technique in improv, in a corporate environment, "yes, and" is an inviting and easy way to own the next step or pursue the next connection in a conversation. It provides anyone who's tried it with a clear physical and emotional sense of what it feels like to be okay in a conversation that you don't know where it's going. It builds your muscle memory—when repetition over time gives you the ability to exercise with little or no conscious effort—around confidence in conversational interactions, and it's a proven tool to deliver steady footing for engaging on just about any topic whatsoever.

Collaborative Solution Building

Notes are the closing ritual of every rehearsal. It's the time when the director, the entire cast, and the design team sit together to discuss how the performance went, examining what worked, what didn't, why, and what might yet be done. It's the creative equivalent of performance feedback in real time. It's immediate and relevant and is delivered with an expectation of ownership and proactive solution building. Cast members rely on this ritual to hone performance. This isn't to say there isn't pushback. But this expected and productive form of engagement and questioning is the bedrock of effective collaboration. A director cannot give a note about an actor's awkward movement on stage and not honor the actor who may be struggling with a costume issue that prohibits the expected movement. The costume designer comes into the conversation to help determine how the end goal can be achieved without too much compromise of either costume design or effects. How could he move differently to get the effect the director wants? How can the costume be modified? How important is the movement effect to the scene? All of these questions are on the table, which is also to say that no one questions the intention of the note. This level of openness is critical to feedback, to problem-solving solutions, and to the ability to build cohesive teams.

Role-Play

The whole idea of theater is to step into another person's shoes to perform a role, to embody their story and perspective, and to see how they see and speak how they speak. Actors sustain this skill for a full show; as an organizational learning tool, managers only need to do it for a few minutes. Role-playing demands that you change your frame in how you think or approach a situation. Even within those few minutes, role-play can be eye-opening. When others watch you, they see themselves and the flaws, both obvious and subtle, that are surfaced. And when we are actively engaged in role-playing, we can understand *why* we get the kind of responses we get from our employees. We realize how we are speaking to them, and we can feel the difference immediately, especially when we are attempting to speak in ways we do not normally engage. Role-play is the best practice forum for accountability. It is your communication gym, the place where you work out your approach to performance issues.

Let's strip out the drama from your thinking about performance as a leader or manager or teammate. Let's reduce the stress and eliminate the pain and frustration we all go through when things don't come out as expected and when people let us down. Accountability should be an everyday kind of conversation—not a conversation reserved for moments when something has gone horribly wrong or when daily infractions have piled up so high they can no longer be ignored. These conversations can and should happen in the hallway on the way to or from a meeting; they're not a formal event that needs tons of planning and preparation. Yes, this book will ensure that you'll be prepared and have thought about that conversation, but you'll also understand that preparation is not an eight-week

> Role-play is the best practice forum for accountability. It is your communication gym, the place where you work out your approach to performance issues.

process. And the more you practice, the faster you'll be able to prepare—so much so that you'll be able to have these conversations on the fly when you need to.

I hinted earlier that many organizations have taken on the terms *crucial* and *fierce* as monikers for conversations focused on accountability. To a certain extent, I agree. I believe, for example, that *Crucial Conversations* is a fantastic book with excellent information to guide you through *high-stakes* conversations when relationships are at risk. The same holds true for the book *Fierce Conversations*, which addresses situations in which you've got to stand in your values in the moment, in whatever circumstances have given rise to drama. But I want to promise you this: if you practice accountability every day, you will reduce the need for anything *fierce* or *crucial*. Your ability to create clarity and own your expectations will trump the drama all day long.

Get in the ring, and get a little sweaty. I dare you.

In this book, it's my intent to double down on the reference to Theodore Roosevelt's "Citizenship in a Republic" speech that Brené Brown references in her book *Daring Greatly*:

> It is not the critic who counts; not the man who points out how the strong man stumbles, or where the doer of deeds could have done better. The credit belongs to the man who is actually in the arena, whose face is marred by dust and sweat and blood; who strives valiantly; who errs, who comes short again and again because there is no effort without error and shortcoming; but who dares actually strive to do the deeds; who knows great enthusiasms, the great devotions; who spends himself in a worthy cause; who as the best knows in the end the triumph of high achievement, and who at the worst if he fails, at least fails while daring greatly so that his place shall never be with those cold and timid souls who neither know victory nor defeat.[5]

Brown uses Roosevelt's words to engender her baseline understanding of vulnerability: Vulnerability is the courage to get in there and do life.[6]

It's in *doing* that I have learned all the lessons about accountability that I share with you in this book. I know from experience that accountability is an act of vulnerability, which is why the doing of it is so daunting. And because I've been shoulder to shoulder with hundreds of managers who dare to learn, practice, and apply accountability with others at work, I am intimately engaged with the struggle, the stumbling, the dust, and the sweat. I have learned from so many stories of the trials and tribulations that managers encounter every day with other people at work. And although I'm here to tell you that

---

5   Brené Brown, *Daring Greatly: How the Courage to Be Vulnerable Transforms the Way We Live, Love, Parent and Lead* (Avery, 2012), p. 1.

6   I realize the Roosevelt quote, while historic and very fitting for Brown's sentiment as well as mine, is not inclusive. Go ahead and read your "she's" into that—mostly because "she" has to dare twice as hard and maybe even twice as much.

we overdramatize the amount of dust, sweat, and blood to expect, I still want to recognize and honor the fact that accountability remains a vulnerable act. That's why Roosevelt's words, and Brown's recalling of them, remain significant to me. I want to inspire you to be bold, to dare greatly in your everyday encounters. But I also want you to know that your ability to be completely successful *doing* accountability —with everyone you need to and on a regular basis—is completely within your grasp.

It's my passion for communication as an art form and my intimacy with language from a performance standpoint that have convinced me that conversation is an action and that it embodies our relationships. My training and my passion for performance have enabled me to work with people to develop the practice—and the art—of better communication for more powerful and more lasting outcomes.

My Accountability Habits Were Homegrown

My work in corporate training and coaching is also intimately connected to family, friendships, and other close relationships. In a sense, I've been trained in this work all my life—which might explain why I believe that accountability ultimately starts at home.

There is a long and steady history in my family emphasizing taking responsibility for yourself and your actions. Growing up, it was a given that when you made a commitment to do something, you did it. Now, with my own children, we refer to this as "sticking to the deal." For us, it's a tribal rule. You don't say you'll get all your chores done before leaving to hang out with your friends and then change your mind when you get a call to go do something fun earlier than planned. Instead, you tell your friend you've got to get your chores done first. If you're clever, you learn to enlist your friends to come help you, so you can go have fun earlier than scheduled. That might sound simple and quaint—

something all good parents do. But they don't—at least not consistently. And consistency is part of the recipe for habits of accountability to stick. It's the "stickiness" in *sticking to the deal.*

What I know now, after growing up in the family that I did, after raising two children, and after training and coaching hundreds of managers, is that my inclinations and understanding around accountability began at a very young age with my own parents insisting on sticking to the deal and coming clean when you screwed up. I learned early on that accountability isn't just about what you're *going* to do; it's also about what you did or didn't do. I did a lot of cleanup when I didn't come home in time to let the dog out. I spent some weekends at home when I missed my curfew. I lost my car keys when I drove too many friends at once. *Conversations were had.* They were not fun. They were not easy, but they occurred every time, consistently. Consequences followed. And while at the time there may have been some adolescent resentment on my part, I did get over it.

> I learned early on that accountability isn't just about what you're *going* to do; it's also about what you did or didn't do.

Don't get me wrong—my parents were not disciplinarians. They were fun; they still are. But they did not shy away when those important conversations were necessary. There was no "wait until your father gets home." Feedback was immediate, unless there was too much anger, in which case we spoke when rational sensibilities returned—something that can happen surprisingly fast.

I was also accustomed at an early age to understand that accountability is personal. My offenses were not just the breaking of abstract rules; they were transgressions against my mother's or my father's wishes and expectations. Serious as that might sound, it meant that

I was never afraid of my parents or worried about what they'd do if I transgressed the rules. There was always clarity. I knew when I was crossing a line or not sticking to the deal. I knew when I was making a bad decision. And as I got older and more independent, that just raised the stakes of the game when it came to weighing the consequences of my actions.

When it came to enforcing accountability, my parents did not disappoint—at the kitchen table, during dinner, in the car, at the grocery store, at the movies, in front of my friends; wherever we were when feedback was needed, they rose to the occasion. They met my eyeballs with a practical conversation designed to guide me back toward more responsible and appropriate behavioral choices. They did their best to positively influence my decision-making and my actions, all the while standing behind me with full support, even at the worst of times.

I've come to understand that not everyone has this sort of experience during their formative years. As I came into the professional arena and began to pay close attention to how people choose to behave and take action, I found myself aggravated by others who had a tendency not to *stick to the deal*. I was amazed at how common it was, how easy it was for some people to look outside of themselves for any excuse not to deliver what they had promised or were being paid to do. So, like most, I got frustrated, even angry, but I lived with it.

What else could I do?

Then began my career in training development and design, a path I followed after my theater career, apprenticed to my mother who was a lifelong teacher, first in high school American history then in adult education for nonprofits and eventually corporations. From her, again, I learned that the very question "What else can I do?" was already a way of avoiding accountability. Joining my mother's thriving training enterprise, I learned firsthand about collaboration, accountability, and timely product delivery in corporate environments. As it turned out, my mother and I had very complementary skill sets for designing and delivering behavior change through corporate training programs.

Over the next ten years, she and I, along with the help of my brother and eventually my father—I may have mentioned that accountability was strong in our family—worked on testing and perfecting management trainings in interpersonal communication skills.

My mother and I both knew intuitively that one-and-done wasn't ever good enough. From our own commitment to "sticking to the deal" for our clients, we knew we needed to deliver something that really shifted behaviors and measurably improved skills. We were able to innovate highly impactful skills training and performance development techniques that I am still using, and improving, today—some thirty-plus years later.

Here's the Deal

Accountability was our thing—not just as a family standard and operating principle but as a focus for trainings that we shared across the globe. We understood intuitively that no matter where we worked, what clients we had, what industry those clients were in, one primary source of pain for every organization was the struggle around driving accountability with employees and teams, leaders, and managers. "There's no accountability here" is a sentence that's literally heard around the world.

We chose to dissect what we did as a family and how we did it to see if there was something there that we could share with clients at a professional level. The result of that effort is the OwnUp! program. It's been tested, improved, and validated by thousands of managers in multiple countries. It's the foundation of that program that I share with you here. I want you to experiment with it and begin your own practice for holding yourself and others accountable every day.

To help you up your game, I'll guide you through three shifts (see figure 1). These shifts are an expansion of your thinking about results, what people did or didn't do, and the tasks that need to be completed to get you back to the results you wanted in the first place. Yes! You want to think about that in terms of accountability, and you also want to approach it from a people-first perspective to include how things are done or not done, as well as what needs to change and how you help your people develop so as not to keep going around in circles on performance issues. We start with Part I: Value Shift. This section of the book asks you to check your head on how you think about accountability, how it's really defined, and why your approach to it matters. It's the part where we set up the rules of the game and have a look at the playing arena. Part II: Skill Shift lays out a model I call the Six Ownership Steps (or S.O.S.) and walks you through each step that you would apply in an effective accountability conversation. Part II is what you do when you're in the arena; this is where all the drama—the dust and sweat and blood—might occur. Of course, you'll want to skip right to Part II because that's why you picked up this book. *Don't do it.* When you shortcut Part I, chances are you'll suck at Part II and can continue to expect mostly blood from your encounters. You can't jump to excellence in conversation when you haven't taken time to unpack all your bags around accountability in the first place. Part III: Time Shift explains how true ownership for performance includes ownership for needed change and improvement as well. Taking up the skill set of a manager-as-coach really is like watching your arena footage to see what specific strategies and changes are needed to win.

EXPAND YOUR THINKING

GETTING TO "YES, AND..."

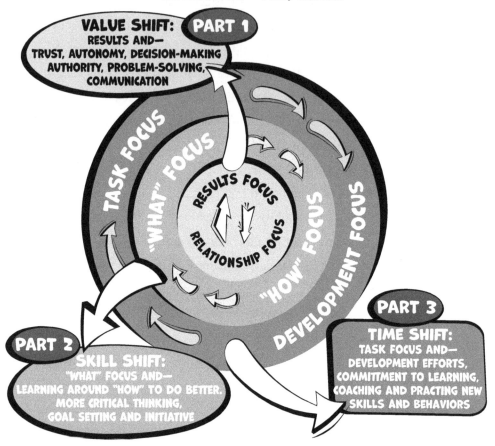

Figure 1

So I strongly recommend you read the entirety of this book in the order it's presented. You'll save yourself the awkward experience of the moment you realize you should have done that to begin with. Reconsider your urge to shortcut the process and trust me to take you through it step by step.

PART I
Value Shift

EXPAND YOUR THINKING

GETTING TO "YES, AND..."

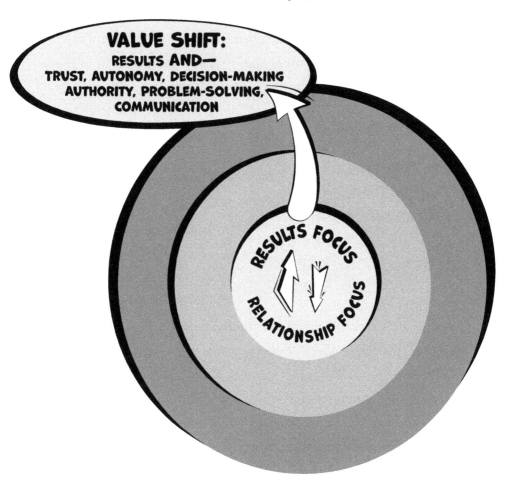

Figure 2

ACCOUNTABILITY IS one of those words we all know and use but a skill that very few practice with any consistency. Accountability is about managing relationships. It's not a process so much as it's what sits between people. It is not punitive. It is not a consequence, and it is not justice. *Accountability is an act of clarity.* Its only outcome is clarity around ownership of either actions or inactions and of the choices associated with those actions or inactions.

> *Accountability is an act of clarity.* Its only outcome is clarity around ownership of either actions or inactions and of the choices associated with those actions or inactions.

We're all too familiar with current challenges to the practice of accountability. On the one hand, there's the demand that there be more of it, and on the other hand, in more extreme cases, there's demand for *some* accountability where there has been none. We know the long history of the absence of corporate accountability, which includes the Enron debacle, the ExxonMobil Valdez and the BP Deepwater Horizon spills, and the Volkswagen emissions shenanigans. More recently there's been account fraud at Wells Fargo, Cambridge Analytica and Facebook scandals, and Boeing 737 MAX crashes. These and other examples like them stand out among circumstances in which there has been sustained clamoring for people and organizations to take responsibility for their choices, words, and actions. The very scale and depth of many of these issues can make accountability seem exhausting, frustrating, time-consuming, and even impossible. However, accountability is exactly the right rallying cry for when we've all had enough.

We've all been let down and disappointed in what we've expected from our leaders, peacekeepers, legislators, schools, workplaces, and—for some—our families, neighbors, and friends. We are living through a time when everyone seems to be running amok with their blame-throwers all fired up, torching whomever and whatever they see fit. Intuitively, we know that we need more accountability, that there has never been a more appropriate time for developing and enforcing it. But—and given the fact that we haven't seen enough of it lately in public life—what exactly does accountability look like? And do we have any idea of the practical steps we might take to achieve it?

Given the wide scope of its applicability in work and in life, accountability is one of the most powerful skill sets you will ever master. It's a character-defining practice that touches everything—every single relationship you have. When you master accountability, you find your center as a person, you lay a critical foundation for how you show up in the world and how you can deal with that world more effectively. Mastering accountability gives you the understanding and the power to make your life better, which, in turn, has the benefit of making the lives of those around you better too.

For that reason, the most important thing you need to know at the start of this book is that *accountability starts with you.* That may not be what you want to hear. But it's the truth of the matter, a truth that I'll work to convince you of as you read through the chapters that follow.

> Mastering accountability gives you the understanding and the power to make your life better, which, in turn, has the benefit of making the lives of those around you better too.

I'm guessing the reason you picked up this book is because, like the rest of us, you struggle to get accountability right, either personally or organizationally, or both. If that's so, consider yourself among the brightest minds in human resources and organizational development who have been working to understand this topic for years.

The increased pace of change (and corresponding pressure) within our work environments has brought issues of accountability to the fore. First, there was attention paid to people management more broadly than before. With that came the utilization of accountability conversations as an exercise for aligning performance to organizational goals; in other words, accountability was understood to be part of performance management. These conversations typically occurred as part of performance review, which for many is once or twice a year. The primary outcome of these conversations, however, was being ranked and rated. Then there was a more radical shift within some organizations. Performance management came to be understood more as an ongoing development tool with a focus on helping people perform better in their roles and grow in their careers. To quote Josh Bersin, an expert and researcher in the field as well as a principal at Bersin by Deloitte:

> While all this technological change has been occurring—taking us to the precipice of a major change in platforms (from cloud to mobile)—there has also been a major shift in business focus. Today, companies are far less focused on automating and integrating their talent practices. Instead, they are worried about employee engagement, teamwork, innovation, and collaboration.... The real focus is on reinventing how people work; creating team-based tools for goal alignment and coaching; putting in place systems to provide feedback and measure engagement; and rethinking the way we measure performance, manage careers, and enable individual learning. Overall, we see this as a shift from the integrated talent management practices of the early 2000s to the people management concerns of today.[7]

7　Josh Bersin, "HR Technology Disruptions for 2017: Nine Trends Reinventing the HR Software Market," Bersin by Deloitte, Perspective 2016, https://www.ig.cl/wp-content/uploads/2016/11/HR-Technology-trends-2016-by-Bersin.pdf.

Today, we even have full three-day business conferences on how to *work human*. Gallup has pioneered a data revolution based on measuring employee engagement, and companies are focused on understanding cultural challenges and management mindsets in order to glean a stronger human capital strategy. In 2020, Gary Hamel, a deep and influential thinker and writer on management and organizational structures in business, put out a book called *Humanocracy: Creating Organizations as Amazing as the People Inside Them*, which focuses on reinventing management, flipping the proverbial pyramid—the top-down organizational structure also known as "command and control"—and giving more people ownership, control, and freedom within organizations.

My claim in this book is that the very ideas behind these sorts of changes situate accountability as a prerequisite at every level. You need accountability for performance in order to achieve any of the human capital outcomes your business is aiming for. That's to say, you need accountability to be done well and consistently. For that to occur, the first thing you'll likely need to do is shift your values.

CHAPTER 1

Accountability in Context

EVERYTHING I'M SHARING with you is perfectly applicable outside the workplace (at home, with your kids, with volunteer organizations, and the like), but my focus here is on the business application of accountability practices. We spend most of our time at work, and whether we are managers, leaders, or individual contributors on a team, the opportunity to practice accountability comes almost daily. Depending on the size of your team and the performance pressure you're under, that opportunity might come almost hourly. As you develop excellence in driving accountability, you'll see how these skills essentially become part of who you are and how you roll. Accountability will stop becoming something you *have to do* in order to get *the important stuff* done or deliver results. It will stop being a chore. You'll no longer feel insecure or trepidatious about how to deal with difficult people or tough situations that threaten project success or the achievement of desired results.

Your ability to apply the knowledge and skills I'll share with you here will take the heartache out of *negative* feedback and give you confidence to stand in the moment and purposefully build trust. That will create better work relationships, as well as better teamwork and stronger overall alignment. Ultimately, accountability is a powerful and positive skill set that positions you as a powerful and positive professional.

As with everything relative to success, you'll have to work at it—more so in the beginning, less so after it becomes a habit. Most important, you'll have to acknowledge that practicing accountability is a choice. You either choose to master it or you don't and accept that you'll go on doing the same things you've always done, still expecting a different result.

> Ultimately, accountability is a powerful and positive skill set that positions you as a powerful and positive professional.

It's a Downshift, Not an Upshift

Here's where the issue of a values shift becomes relevant. Not until you situate accountability as a central focus of your management practice will you reap the benefits. When you downshift, you gain traction and control. If you're going to increase your speed to results, you must downshift when taking the curves and corners. Dealing with accountability is akin to cornering before you hit the straightaway. Taking that second to shift slows you down and offers you a second to strategize before you hit the gas. It's a moment to recognize what's most important in your next move.

Immediate Gain and Better Execution

When you shift from ignoring, avoiding, or postponing on the one hand to belittling, humiliating, and punishing bad behaviors, poor choices, and disappointing results on the other, you'll value facing performance issues as they occur. To the extent that you come to value clarity, curiosity, and composure in those conversations, your gains in performance will come faster and easier. Your employees' ability to execute will increase.

Better Credibility, Personally and Organizationally

Generally speaking, your technical and subject matter expertise no longer matters when you become a manager or leader. Your experience in those areas, while useful from a coaching perspective, is no longer as critical as your ability to manage the people who report to you. You can have all the technical know-how in the world, but if you allow underperformers to consistently underdeliver, if you do not address performance issues and unmet expectations effectively and in a timely manner, you are no longer credible, no matter how great your past experience and depth of technical knowledge. So no accountability = no results = no cred. When you shift to valuing relationships over expertise, you'll move toward greater credibility among those you're responsible for managing.

Reduced Rework and/or Work-Arounds

Accountability begins with clarity of expectations. Greater clarity drives better decision-making and fewer mistakes from your team members, and that increases your chances of getting things right the first time. My manufacturing colleagues, for example, know that first-time quality is critical for cost savings, but the insight applies across the board, regardless of your specific industry. My point here also applies both to business profitability and to achieving a desirable business culture.

Accountability will also lead to less of a requirement to *work around* other people. When I say *work around*, I'm not talking about a technical process. I'm talking about dealing with people who are regularly referred to as *difficult, toxic, retired in place, not a team player*, or *blame shifters*. You know these people, and you know how they can be shifted around within an organization, going from group to group, department to department. These are the people we learn to work around because we can't seem to get them to step up to the plate in a functional and meaningful way. Instead of dealing with them, we invent ways to work around them. Using accountability to solve the dilemma of the work-around leads to cost savings, as well as improvements in company culture.

Increased Productivity and Less Organizational Cost

In their book *An Everyone Culture: Becoming a Deliberately Developmental Organization*, Robert Kegan and Lisa Laskow Lahey diagnose a problem that plagues organizations in which accountability is not part of daily work life. They write:

> In an ordinary organization, most people are doing a second job no one is paying them for. In businesses large and small … people are spending time and energy covering up their weaknesses, managing other people's impressions of them, showing themselves to their best advantage, playing politics, hiding their inadequacies, hiding their uncertainties, hiding their limitations. Hiding.

To this they add:

> We regard this as the single-biggest loss of resources that organizations suffer every day.… The total cost of this waste is simple to state and staggering to contemplate: it prevents organizations and the people who work in them from reaching their full potential.[8]

In the world of workplace performance accountability, we describe this sort of *hiding* as denial of ownership or an unwillingness to be accountable for workplace performance decisions, an unwitting choice to adhere to hidden cultural or personal objectives (serving our fears instead of our potential)—a practice that results

---

8   Robert Kegan and Lisa Laskow Lahey, *An Everyone Culture: Becoming a Deliberately Developmental Organization* (Harvard Business Review Press, 2016), 1.

in a costly cultural norm for many organizations. It's a momentum killer. When you shift from valuing fear to valuing potential, you'll create momentum. Accountability removes the need for *hiding*, which begets better decision-making and better outcomes. Best of all, a shift in productivity can happen as the result of a single conversation.

Increased Trust and Reliability

Trust is the holy grail of workplace culture because it's so foundational for our connectivity as human beings. You have an opportunity to build trust with every conversation you have and every behavior after the fact. Trust is complex, just as relationships are complex. It requires the work of two: the trusting and the trustworthy. It denotes dependability and reliability and is created through interactions and behaviors that match statements and intentions. Trust is far less fragile than we believe it to be, and it can be cultivated faster than we think. Practicing accountability on a daily basis builds both trust and respect faster. Higher trust drives higher productivity because less time is spent double-checking, waiting for action or decisions, and dealing with lip service or malicious compliance and other interpersonal problems such as blaming, criticizing, and the like. When you value trust over doubt and manipulation, you'll internally motivate and engage employees. Mistakes will undoubtedly be made, but when there is trust, there is a reliable way forward through learning and problem-solving.

Higher Engagement

With accountability practices firmly in place, you can purposefully achieve higher engagement, meaning more personal investment in a job or task, as well as in the organization as a whole. The effects of engagement include reduced turnover, enthusiasm, commitment, and willingness to go the extra mile. When employees have clarity about expectations, they know what to do, and when they get useful feedback, they know *how* they're doing. These simple-sounding details allow them to take actions and make decisions that are better for themselves, the department, and the business as a whole. They are allowed to achieve, to learn through failure, and to keep trying because they are supported and therefore motivated to do so.

A Better Business

Accountability is a challenge that lives at every level of management. There are nuances in the way the skills are applied that differ from frontline manager to senior executive, but the baseline skills remain the same.

One manager who is excellent at driving and holding accountability is a good thing. But imagine what can happen if your entire management team gets better at driving and holding others accountable—not just their direct reports but peer to peer, as well as up-line. Better accountability means better clarity and communication, which mean better relationships, more loyalty, less turnover, higher productivity, and happier employees. A dynamic performance culture can only be achieved and sustained if it's supported by a managerial performance standard centered around accountability. By establishing solid baseline skills around accountability, you build a performance standard for your managers—the stewards who deliver your performance culture.

Accountability Myths

With all the benefits we might reap from making accountability a regular practice in our workplaces, what keeps us from adopting it?

In my work with managers, I consistently hear three stories they tell themselves as a means of withdrawing from driving accountability. Make no mistake, these three stories are myths—the kind of tales we tell to explain things we are afraid of and don't really understand. These myths are also a handy excuse for not putting in the effort to change our understanding and behavior. We use these stories to rationalize our inaction and our unwillingness to shift our values.

Myth #1: People are unpredictable— it will all go terribly wrong.

Are they? Will it? I would argue most people are, in fact, very predictable. If anything, the more I've come to understand the workings of the human mind, the more I've found it a little disturbing, at times, just how predictable people are. For example, if you use a smartphone of some kind, have you ever had that moment where you get in the car and the digital assistant lets you know how many minutes it is until you reach your next destination? "Five minutes to get home" she announces, and you're thinking, *Wait, that's not on my calendar, but of course that's where I'm heading ... how does she know?* Even search engines have mastered finishing your thought in the search bar. The robots know we are predictable.

In communication practice, when you really think it through and imagine an accountability conversation in detail, you'll find that you can pretty much guess how someone is most likely to respond to you (unless you truly don't know them at all). And even if they are new to you, accountability conversations are one of the best ways to find out who they are, and fast.

Myth #2: It's complex and futile— some people just won't change.

The best way to let ourselves off the hook is to indulge uncertainty about whether our efforts will actually improve anything. We can feel as if we're up against long-term behavior patterns and that old dogs will not learn new tricks. In coaching terms, we call this an attitude of apathy or complacency. What I say to you, as your coach, is that doing *something* is always better than doing nothing. Doing nothing is what's brought this false story about futility to the surface in the first place.

I've noticed that this myth is particularly prevalent in large organizations with a long-standing culture. It's part of why culture eats strategy for lunch; we *let* it happen by abdicating our efforts to learn and change ourselves, our mindsets, and our approaches. We become victims. We deny the full range of our choices and thereby significantly limit our actions.

Myth #2 is the reason why I emphasize that accountability starts with you. For example, if you believe that accountability is confrontational or punitive and you are averse to conflict or negativity, you will continuously choose to put the conversation off or not have it at all, and you'll find whatever supporting reasons you need to justify your decision. Or if you don't have a particularly negative perception of accountability, you may still see other managerial responsibilities as more important and thereby give short shrift to having the very accountability conversations that would ultimately keep everyone on track.

Myth # 3: You have to *demand* accountability.

Ownership is something that must be taken. It cannot be forced. To put it another way, you can give people responsibilities. However, you cannot expect them to act on those unless they accept those responsibilities. Accountability requires acceptance of choices and results. Insisting on it will achieve something like when the *blue screen of death* appears and your computer stops working—no one hears your screams. Every performance issue you currently have remains yours until ownership and accountability are otherwise taken through a conversation that creates clarity.

Accountability Is a Mindset and a Skill Set

As I pointed out earlier, accountability is a term much bandied about in corporate settings to describe something we find both necessary and missing: *"Well, if we had more accountability from IT, this project might be further along,"* or *"What we're going to need to really turn this around is much greater accountability from our managers and their teams."* Although everyone who's present when these statements are made will nod their heads furiously in agreement as if to say, "About time!" and "Amen to that!" most people don't take the time to really think through what we mean when we request, demand, or require "accountability." Some are angry, frustrated, or disappointed and seeking something more like consequences after the fact: *"People will be held accountable for this!"* Others sense that oversight is lax and seek better management. Mostly, people just want work to get done, to be done correctly, and to be shared relatively evenly.

Let me state this again: Accountability is not punitive; it is not a consequence. It is not justice. *Accountability is an act of clarity.* Its only outcome is clarity around ownership of either actions or inactions and of the choices associated with those actions or inactions. Accountability is clarity of ownership. Clarity of ownership tells us who is responsible for fixing what's wrong and making it right.

Accountability is the basis of a mutual agreement we make when we show up to do the work.

Ideally, consequences are the *product* of accountability (and not the other way around). If you have a culture of accountability, you also have a firm grip on consequences. In other words, without

> Accountability is clarity of ownership. Clarity of ownership tells us who is responsible for fixing what's wrong and making it right.

33

consequences, there is no accountability—not really, and certainly not consistently. That said, what we often find in our work environments is that there are consequences without accountability, as when management uses the weight of consequences as a motivator for accountability, wielding those consequences like a stick to dominate, shame, and blame. Consequences are what result—the "now what?"—when acceptance or responsibility is denied.

To the contrary of that approach, I'm going to arm you with a people-forward approach to accountability rooted first in values and mindset and then applied as a skill set. That's because excellence in accountability is equally both a mindset and a skill set—and it's ultimately expressed as consistent behavior.

Together, we'll reframe and understand accountability as it *should* be practiced in the workplace. Reframing is a necessary part of changing your practice around accountability—it makes acquiring and using the accountability skill set that I'll share in Part II a whole lot easier. Here's what I mean: most of us think accountability is a good thing, but not many of us act on it *as a value*. Our values are what we use as astringent when things are tough or going badly; they're the guardrails that keep us on track. Many of us cannot achieve accountability in the moment, because we have not really made accountability a value that strongly influences our *mindset* or *approach* to action.

Accountability Is Two-Sided

At its core, accountability is personal; it's a relationship between two people. Even among members of a team, accountability sits between each player as an agreement between individuals. For accountability to exist, there must be the same understanding between the two. There are two sides that work together to create the accountability dynamic (expectations and consequences), and there are two levels to the skill itself (fundamental and advanced). Ultimately, accountability is both a basic skill—in the sense that it's absolutely foundational for any effective manager to create trust-based and consistent productivity—and an advanced communication skill—in the sense that mastering it involves developing a capacity for clear and direct communication. If this book succeeds, it will give you more depth of understanding and greater ability for achieving accountability.

Accountability is not mysterious. It's not a gray or fuzzy concept. You'll know when you have it, and you'll know when you don't.

Accountability Transforms Negative Experiences into Positive Ones

In his 2016 book, *The Subtle Art of Not Giving a F#ck: A Counterintuitive Approach to Living a Good Life*, Mark Manson writes the following: "The desire for more positive experience is itself a negative experience. And, paradoxically, the acceptance of one's negative experience is itself a positive experience." Yes, it's a brain twister. But think about it: it's a positive experience to accept one's negative experience, but a negative experience to desire only more positive experience. I think Manson's insight, the whole hilarious tome in fact, really captures the paradox that arises when it comes to taking personal responsibility, especially for our mistakes.

We all know how it feels to screw up. We've all *been there* when it comes to missed deadlines, lost deals, mistakes, underestimations, miscalculations, and misunderstandings. Wishing things were different, hoping it'll all be okay, or hoping that no one will notice or say anything is the same as desiring that positive experience. In and of itself, doing so usually amounts to a negative experience. But when you manage to stand in the moment and own it—when you accept your negative experience—you feel the personal power, even relief, that comes from being accountable. You retain your center. You gain an ability to remain confident. You keep your self-respect. Most important, you learn and grow as a result. You may experience a sense of humility, but that's exactly what you need to activate learning. The very act of owning your mistakes is the foundation of personal power and the very essence of the positivity that you need in order to move forward as an individual and a professional.

When there is a lack of accountability, there is drama. Drama is a great distraction. It demands our attention and sucks away the precious resources of time and energy. Drama can easily take over and feed on all the negative emotional energy that's generated. Drama, and the lack of ownership that precipitates it, also keeps you stuck. It keeps you stuck in a job you don't want, stuck with a boss you hate, stuck in an emotional spiral of dissatisfaction, disappointment, and frustration. Lack of ownership results in drama, precisely because you refuse to learn. But the humility that activates our ability to learn draws us away from drama and toward real possibility for positive change. It's learning that helps us adapt as we go, as well as remain relevant and valuable.

> ## Lack of ownership results in drama, precisely because you refuse to learn.

Now imagine a whole group of people raising the level of accountability with you. Imagine if all your employees could stand in their mistakes and misunderstandings and take a position of ownership right off the bat. That's more than half the battle, right? Think of it like this: behaviors are the unspoken cultural cues in the workplace. When accountability is something that everyone does, it gets a lot easier for everyone to do. We all know that changing the culture of your workplace can happen reasonably fast when you work at scale. But the thing we often forget when it comes to accountability is a point I've made already and will make again before you reach the end of this book: *accountability starts with you.*

Accountability behaviors are like the seeds you plant within yourself first in order to be able to nurture the same behaviors among your team; they can grow exponentially as long as you water them with intention and consistency. Again, accountability isn't something you do *to* others, and it is especially not something you *force* others to do. It always begins with your ability to take ownership first. You can change your culture if you change yourself.

Let's do better. Let's find that power and personal strength. Most of all, let's get some relief from the blame game drama and the denial of poor performance that can make work suck.

CHAPTER 2

The *Act* of Accountability

IN ITS FULLEST SENSE, accountability is three things:

1. A mindset about emotional risk

2. A communication skill set

3. A practice

So why is it so hard to drive accountability? We are afraid, and if not afraid, then uncomfortable. The number one reason it's so difficult is the vulnerability that accompanies emotional risk.

Accountability Is an Emotional Risk

Holding someone else accountable can generate fear and anxiety for some. It can feel like standing on a cliff with a "go" or "no go" decision needing to be made. But as my favorite researcher/maven of shame and author of great books like *Dare to Lead* and *Daring Greatly*, Brené Brown, says, let's "embrace the suck."

Brown defines vulnerability as "the emotion that we experience during times of uncertainty, risk, and emotional exposure."[9] Holding someone to account can feel like we're exposing ourselves, and to be clear, we *are* doing just that. Accountability requires you to take an emotional risk, to be vulnerable, to stand in the moment armed solely

---

9   Brené Brown, *Dare to Lead: Brave Work. Tough Conversations. Whole Hearts* (Random House, 2018), 20.

with your perspective, your experience, and your language skills. To understand more about that risk, let's review some emotions that can come to the fore when we are anticipating or engaging in accountability conversations.

FEAR of the Unknown, of Uncertainty, and of Risk

As humans, we are wired to be afraid of the unknown. Our brains spend most of their time helping to determine if we are safe or not safe. When it comes to conversations in which we are in a position of having to drive accountability, we tend to be in an emotional state. We are more in tune with what we are feeling, especially our own disappointment, frustration, or anger about what did or did not happen. For some, those feelings can be compounded by anxiety or worry. For many of us, our ego is in overdrive, and we are freaked out at the thought of how much the person we are holding accountable might hate us later. Here's the thing: high emotion can cloud our thinking and keep us from being clear about the rationale for the accountability conversations we want to have. In other words, thinking clouded by fear can confuse our answer to the important question: What exactly was the expectation that was not met?

Often, we do not take the time to reflect on this question deeply enough before we feel compelled to confront or address it. Alternately, maybe we've overthought it and have been hanging on to our answer for far too long. This is why accountability conversations—when they're actually happening—can feel so unwieldy; you can end up discussing things you did not anticipate would come up.

Those half ideas and assumptions on the one hand, and over-stuffed histories on the other, can effectively increase feelings of uncertainty. In conversation, some of us might display "fight and protect" behavior, which we call *being defensive* or *insensitive*, while others might have a "freeze and appease" response, in which we tolerate and accommodate whatever our conversation partner has to say. At the management level, we might witness behaviors such as bulldozing or avoidance. Managers who bulldoze think "It's not that hard," or "I don't have time for this," and then run roughshod over their employees. Managers who avoid think "Maybe it'll work itself out," or "It's not that big of a deal," and then either ignore the problem or prepare insufficiently to address the real concerns. No matter the precise expression, all of these reactions stem from distress about potential conflict.

That fear of the unknown has within it a kernel of truth: we *can't* know exactly what's going on with the other person, especially in terms of their potential reactions to what we have to tell them—to the *negative information* they believe they are about to receive. That fear can be exacerbated if we already have a strong sense of a person's *high maintenance* status; maybe there have been experiences in the past in which they have behaved in an emotionally reactive or defensive manner. That, alone, may give us reason to expect that this person will either take constructive feedback personally (and see themselves as a victim) or place the blame on someone or something else (which is also a form of seeing themselves as a victim). But to expect the conveyance of constructive criticism to yield negative reactions and/ or outcomes and then think "Why poke the bear? Ugh!" or to have weak conversations in which we minimize our message and thereby limit its effectiveness? These are not our best possible responses.

I understand that you may have connected accountability and conflict because that's been your experience. But let's clear this up right here: *accountability is clarity not conflict.*

When you become practiced at accountability, there is no blame and there are no victims. It's not about being merciless. It's about being focused and clear. To quote Brené Brown again, "clear is kind."

EXPOSURE of Inadequacy and Insecurity

Sometimes the emotional risk is based on our own feelings of inadequacy or insecurity around communicating. In that case, we might do one of those two unfortunate things I mentioned earlier: (1) brutalize people with our bluntness because we just want to get it over with or are so impatient or frustrated that we just want to say what needs to be said; or (2) minimize by couching what we really want to say, sugarcoating information so that it feels more friendly. In cases like the latter,

> When you become practiced at accountability, there is no blame and there are no victims.

we never get to the point because we're busy talking around the issue. We can end up diminishing how important the matter is and allow the person we're trying to hold accountable to leave the conversation feeling uncertain about what our problem is and why we were talking to them in the first place. When we minimize, we are also more likely to allow ourselves to get sidetracked on peripheral information and secondary issues that have no real bearing on what we intended to discuss.

Minimizing, like avoiding, is a technique that belongs to what Patrick Lencioni, author of *The Five Dysfunctions of a Team: A Leadership Fable*, refers to as "artificial harmony." Managers don't really say what's on their minds, and employees don't really say what they need to say or express how they really feel about the work or their experience. Have you ever walked away from what you thought was going to be the throw-down conversation where you hold feet to the fire only to realize that you discussed something completely different? Or maybe you walked away with more on your shoulders than you anticipated. You assigned yourself follow-up tasks, essentially putting the issue back in your court. No accountability. No ownership. No change.

The list is long and varied when it comes to our self-perceptions, self-doubts, and other ideas that make us feel exposed and vulnerable: we lack experience in communicating directly; we fear being overpowered by a stronger personality; we fear being perceived as overbearing or micromanaging or unorganized. The antidote to most of these perceptions will come from changes in your mindset and your skill set—how you think about accountability and the extent to which you practice specific skills to engage it directly.

DESIRE for Connection to Others

No one really wants to be the asshole. Really. Assholes in management are just people with intentions and no tools. It's a universal feeling to want to be liked, appreciated, and respected. It's human. We are tribal beings who need the tribe for our very survival. That's true as much *in the wild* as at work. Most of us do not get our work done independently; instead, we rely on teammates and coworkers for success. That can make it feel very counterintuitive to take issue with anyone. It's like risking being exiled from the tribe.

Nevertheless, accountability requires you to put your credibility on the line. It requires you to stand in your values, stick to your guns, and—oh, here's a good one—*follow up*.

Our effectiveness both as managers and leaders in any organization is based on our ability to connect with—and not overpower—others. The goal of our interdependence is to achieve healthy attachments and remain connected to our teams and staff so that we're all working toward the same objectives. If we're failing to connect, it's because we are failing to communicate effectively.

Please don't confuse *connecting* with *liking*. They are not the same thing. You don't have to like everyone who works for you, but you should respect them. People generally stop listening to those who don't respect them, and listening is half the effort when it comes to communicating. Good, open, genuine, and consistent communication is called transparency. Not only does transparency facilitate our connections with others, but it also diminishes fear of the unknown.

NEGATIVITY about Outcomes

The emotional risk that accompanies accountability contributes to one of the myths I mentioned earlier—the belief that accountability conversations will always suck. We are predisposed toward negativity when it comes to accountability because we sense that if you have true accountability, you must also have consequences. However, and ironically, most organizations don't have either, or they've got limited consequences that may be out of proportion to unmet expectations or underperformance. When consequences are for the most part an afterthought, accountability will be varied, at best. Instead of thinking about leveraging consequences as a way to positively frame accountability, we tend to think of them instead as punishment. But there's a critical difference: a punishment is about penalties and retribution, whereas a consequence is an outcome or corollary aftereffect.

> The goal of our interdependence is to achieve healthy attachments and remain connected to our teams and staff so that we're all working toward the same objectives.

Even when we understand that difference, we may still cling to feeling negatively about identifying and enforcing consequences. If you're a parent and you have tried using "time-out" as a tool for disciplining your child, I'm guessing you quickly learned that when Junior is in time-out, everyone is in time-out. This is because you have to pay vigilant attention to Junior during the entirety of time-out. You have to watch and make sure he's not kicking the wall with his dirty shoes to make a point of his feeling about being in time-out, not sneaking off or playing with something while he should be sitting still and reflecting on his behavior. Time-out is a weird—and negatively framed—version of a Performance Improvement Plan. It

> **Punishment is about penalties and retribution, whereas a consequence is an outcome or corollary aftereffect.**

makes a lot of extra work for everyone. It's exhausting. And that sucks. But here's the thing: our negative experiences and perspective come from putting results first and the people second.

To the contrary, when accountability is practiced correctly, it feels *good*. Its central and counterintuitive-seeming demand—that you put people first, instead of results—takes away negative feelings by removing confusion, frustration, and a focus on punitive outcomes.

If you've experienced any of these feelings about practicing accountability—fear, negativity, a sense of exposure, and the like—consider this the beginning of your new story. Accountability is going to become your new secret weapon for gaining personal power, productivity, clarity, and respect—and for leaving all those negative feelings behind.

"Chance favors the prepared mind," said Louis Pasteur, offering an insight that could not be more true than when you put yourself out there and have the conversation. Risk in these conversations happens both in terms of *doing* and *not doing*. You can risk all of these emotions (exposure, connectedness, uncertainty, and negativity) while leveraging your skills and putting yourself formally on the learning curve. This is what I call *learning out loud*. Your discomfort *is* your learning.

Alternately, you can risk (perhaps continue to risk) by doing nothing or by doing things the same way you've always done them. You will reap the consequences of your decision either way. Your choice.

Accountability Is a Communication Skill Set

Accountability is about relationships, and relationships are about communication. I said at the start of this book that I believe your conversations *are* your relationships. The words you choose, the means you use (face-to-face, online, phone, or email), as well as your tone and tenor (how you modulate your voice to emphasize your meaning) and the positioning and motion of your body (how you comport yourself toward your conversation partner)—all of that is reflective of your relationship with that person.

It follows, then, that if you are not speaking to someone, you are not having a relationship with that person. For example, if you are a manager who speaks to your team primarily when things are going badly, you are having the kind of relationship where you are only there to whip people into performing as desired. You are a hammer, and they are the nails. You are demonstrating that you are not invested in them as people. Even if that attitude may not be true from your perspective, and even though you may feel you are speaking and behaving in a supportive manner, your team may be experiencing you otherwise, all because your conversations are limited only to conversations about corrective actions. To the extent that your conversations are limited, so are your relationships, your impact, and your effectiveness.

The goal is to create connection and clarity, and doing so demands that you engage intentionally in having conversations and building relationships no matter your particular communication style—whether you're a "stick to business" communicator, a super friendly one, or somewhere in between.

Communicating with Purpose

Mastering accountability starts and finishes with your ability to communicate well. There are a lot of philosophies about good communication put forth in management training programs and other leadership books. The one thing they all have in common is this: communication done well begins with purpose. That means there is a clear answer to questions like: *What is the purpose of the conversation?* and *Why are we meeting?* Accountability done well is not an *add on*.

You don't bury it in another agenda as an "oh yeah, we should also talk about this" bullet point or unannounced item. Driving accountability for performance

> **Communication done well begins with purpose.**

results is fundamental to business success, and so treating these important conversations as an aside or afterthought communicates that you see business results as an aside or afterthought as well.

Accountability communication is no different than leadership communication inasmuch as you do it for a specific reason and outcome. If I'm going to get buy-in from you about what our division goals are, I'm going to speak to you in a way that is motivating and inspiring. I'm going to compel you with both logic and emotion. I'm going to engage you in dialogue. Likewise, if I'm going to drive accountability, I'm going to create the time and space with you to have that conversation. I'm going to do that because I want to communicate that I care about the results, and I care about you as the person who is struggling to achieve them. I enter every accountability conversation with this intention and without judgment. I assume nothing. I model what I expect. I am clear, and I don't mince words, but I am also careful not to be a bully or deliver a one-sided monologue.

Accountability communication does not just involve the conveyance of information. It's also the connection you build, the dialogue you create, and the resulting actions you inspire. And that includes feelings—how you and the other person feel about what is being said—because feelings are how we remember our conversations. We primarily retain how we felt about them, not so much exactly what was said.

Communication Is a Pattern

Communicating with each other is a fundamental human activity that begins on day one. Our approach and mastery of language and interpersonal communication is very much a product of our upbringing, education, and personality. However, our ability to be effective with it, for a specific purpose, is always in need of improvement. Think about it like this: If you've got to give a presentation, do you want to stand up and repeat the words on your slide deck, or do you want to show up ready to deliver a TED Talk? I'm not saying that driving accountability means you need to be a *master communicator*. I'm saying most people need more focus and specific intentions, as well as effective language in the moment. I'm also arguing that knowing what skills to use and when, how to apply them in the moment, and how to focus on your language takes just a little more effort than you give to most regular conversation.

Given that we all talk every day, sometimes nearly all day, the way we speak tends to be patterned and routine. In other words, we all have a comfort zone when it comes to how we communicate with others. An excellent tool for understanding these comfort zones in behaviors, communication, and relationship styles is a DISC assessment; perhaps you've even taken one (or several). DISC assessments have been around for decades, and there are a lot of variations out there. The most highly validated assessment comes from the original theories developed by Dr. William Moulton Marston in his 1928 book, *Emotions of Normal People*, and currently owned by John Wiley & Sons.

Wiley's version is DiSC, with a lowercase *i* in the name, and is an acronym for the four primary styles: D is for dominant, I is for influence, S is for steadiness, and C is for conscientiousness. As you may be able to deduce from the general style names, each style encompasses a myriad of behaviors and priorities. For example, the D, or dominant style, prioritizes getting immediate results, taking action, and challenging themselves as well as others. They are motivated by power, authority, competition, winning, and success. They come across as confident, direct, sometimes even forceful and risk-taking. Of course, you can be a mix of styles as well.

Assessments are good for individuals and organizations to get a common language and understanding around how everyone tends to communicate and relate. Assessments are also a cornerstone of personal development because you gain insights into your own world. You become more self-aware, and that self-awareness increases your ability to hold yourself accountable. It becomes easier for you to own your own strengths, blind spots, and challenges. I personally use Everything DiSC assessments in our training on accountability skills to enhance understanding and self-awareness about what participants' default comfort zones entail. More important, I use the assessment to help participants understand the three *other* primary comfort zones from the one with which they're most familiar. The idea is that while it's critical to be self-aware regarding your own style habits, it's even more critical to be aware of the other ones so that you can develop the flexibility to *go there* when it makes sense to do so. This is what's called versatility in communication. Increasing versatility in how you make assertions and respond to others is exactly what makes you an effective communicator. And having the additional information and level of self-awareness that comes from having a DISC assessment in your toolbox increases your effectiveness in driving accountability, not to mention your communication and relationships in general. Your communication skill set should involve stretching outside your comfort zone and working within someone else's at the same time that you practice specific communication skills that apply to accountability.

Accountability Is a Practice

I talk about accountability in two primary ways: from a theater perspective and from a yoga perspective. I've already hinted at the ways that theater practices are relevant. In the theater, there's tremendous emphasis on and care for words, the intention or motivation behind them, and their delivery as part of a convincing conversation. I bring yoga to bear because of the ways it emphasizes breath, muscle memory, flexibility, and focus. The depth of your stretch and the integrity of your pose are not always the same every day. Yoga just asks that you be present and make your best effort with your intentions. The same is true for accountability.

Both disciplines—theater and yoga—require a regular effort; rehearsing and practicing daily is what brings mastery and ease. Mastering accountability conversations relies on the same effort—disciplined attempts, followed by learning, correcting, and trying again. And both disciplines require that we move from intellectualizing the process to actually attempting it—a move that's assisted by having good models, directors, teachers, and coaches. It's super helpful to work with someone who can show you how it's done and give you real-time feedback and immediate understanding of how you're actually doing. This is why there are mirrors in a yoga studio and why directors give notes during rehearsals. My standing bow pose, for example, would be very different if I'd just read about it as opposed to taking a class with an instructor who could both show me and offer me real-time feedback and adjustments to improve my form. Similarly, theater rehearsals create space for experimentation guided by a director; they allow all involved to see and hear what works and what doesn't. Until you can walk across the stage with your lines in your mind, clear intentions, and some rehearsal time clocked, your ability to perform in the moment is limited—especially when it comes to being effective and believable.

You can up your performance game very quickly in either theater or yoga with some targeted practice, and the same is true for holding accountability conversations. Merely thinking about what you'll say versus practicing saying those words out loud—verbalizing your thinking—changes everything. We often don't realize, until it's too late, that our *internal conversations*—our brain's version of shorthand—are not the same as conversations with real other people. That's why it can feel remarkably awkward when we take what we're thinking and practice saying it out loud. That opening line may not turn out to be at all what we were expecting to hear. The same sort of thing holds true when you write out bullet points before sharing your thoughts. When you take the language off the page and add breath, tone, pitch, urgency, speed, and all the other paralinguistics and body language into it, does it match your intention? Too often, we're surprised and disappointed by the differences.

From the theater, I want to carry forward and emphasize the value of rehearsing, of focusing in and on the moment and experimenting with language and intention. From yoga, I want to draw your attention to the variability in practice. When it comes to your accountability practice, some days you'll be a rock star, and your verbal agility will be masterful. These will be the days when you're on top of your ability to identify behaviors or results, to analyze them quickly, and then to speak to the situation elegantly. Some days, though, you'll be a little stiff, and you'll have a hard time concentrating on your breath, which will then make it difficult to concentrate on your movements and especially difficult to speak with intention and purpose. When you lose connection to your breath, it's very easy to become distracted by your inner monologue—all the things you say to yourself in the moment that can kill your confidence and focus. When you can't connect to your intentions, you lose your focus. You have conversations that wander. You listen to what's going on in your head instead of to the person you're speaking with. You fail to really hear or confirm what you're hearing. You problem solve issues that are not relevant to the real performance issues you're having. And you take on things you did not intend and may end up feeling very unsatisfied or disappointed that the conversation went nowhere.

Most people fail at mastering accountability because they want to intellectualize the steps and skip the practice, as if any one of us could just walk onto a stage and deliver an admirable performance or teach a yoga class from having looked at a series of images. Most want to approach those conversations as if they could just say the lines and move the story forward (get through the conversation) and get on to the next scene (get to a result or change). But when you recognize that accountability is not a monologue where you deliver all the lines—"and cut; that's a wrap"—when you realize that you're participating in a dialogue that's not fully scripted and that

> **Most people fail at mastering accountability because they want to intellectualize the steps and skip the practice.**

requires responsiveness and *play* back and forth, that's when training and practice start to seem absolutely necessary for success. We must experience and embody the real-time action of the conversation to gain true mastery. And that involves repeated practice and role-play.

Think of it this way: if actors in a play were to rehearse on their own using artificial intelligence or video tapes of other actors who had played the role previously, and then showed up on stage in front of a live audience with other live actors to perform a show, how do you think the performance would go? This is essentially what we are asking of our managers whenever we ask them to learn how to coach employees or drive accountability using e-learning. Even classroom learning provides very limited feedback for behavior change and skill mastery, and that's because training soft skills effectively requires ongoing immediate feedback or input.

Learning provides content and context. It may inspire action. But without real-time feedback, without rehearsal or regular practice, the brain cannot connect the information with the experience and create new, repeatable behaviors with any confidence or consistency. Muscle memory is real, and mastering accountability depends upon it.

CHAPTER 3

Feedback Is One-Third of Accountability

TO DEVELOP A CLEAR PICTURE of accountability, we will need to distinguish it from some related but different categories of communication. Doing so ought to have two results: (1) to show that feedback is one tool of accountability, and (2) to show that accountability is the first, most fundamental shift in a transformative process that also involves coaching.

If you're not clear where performance management stops and developing for improvement begins, how can you be sure you're doing either? Unfortunately, within any given organization, language around performance and how it's addressed is often as much a cultural phenomenon as it is a matter of personal style. We tend to behave in ways that are culturally acceptable within our organizations, especially when we are operating in the roles of leaders and managers. If you're part of an organization that has chosen to use the word *leader* in lieu of *manager*, because the organization's belief is that all managers are leaders, this can actually cause some confusion. No doubt, it's a lovely sentiment, and it might

> If you're not clear where performance management stops and developing for improvement begins, how can you be sure you're doing either?

make some managers feel better about their jobs, but it's not the truth. Managing and leading are different efforts. That isn't to say that one person can't do both; in fact, often they must. But if you're going to be effective at managing performance and driving accountability for that performance, you must be clear in how you speak about it to and within the organization, as much as in the moment of a single conversation.

Managing is primarily a one-to-one relationship focused on delivering expected results. Leading is primarily a one-to-many relationship focused on change. If you were to tell a manager that they are *not leading effectively* in an organization that refers to all managers as leaders, in what part of their role are they underperforming? If you can't effectively name for that manager what she's doing wrong or not doing well, how can she claim it, let alone change it?

In recent years, organizations have invested a lot of money and time into training managers to give feedback and *coach* employees. Yet a lot of those companies are still struggling to *convince* managers to engage in this activity with their direct reports and other employees. The learning and organizational development industry has started to study how well managers are doing when it comes to meeting the increased expectations companies are placing on them to have more frequent feedback conversations. Despite the training and the implementation of software platforms to help remind management and facilitate feedback, the results are not showing the sort or level of gains that were anticipated.

Essentially, the training has done a good job of overwhelming managers and providing them with more emails, chats, reminders, and running comment threads. What it hasn't done is increase engaged conversations that result in ownership and improved performance. I'd argue that *performance* is the most overworked word and underdeveloped commodity in most companies. It's a bit of jargon written on coffee mugs and T-shirts and framed in pictures in the hallway. The challenge is how to actually make the word come alive through actions in which employees choose to develop and apply the appropriate skill at the appropriate level, as well as engage in productive and constructive behavior. The tendency is not only to overtalk *performance* but to overcomplicate it with policies and platforms that achieve very little when it comes to actually changing performance. Exceptional performance is achieved, in reality, one person at a time, through choice.

Ideally, feedback conversations are meant to be meaningful and useful, not just frequent. But many organizations have merely increased the frequency of feedback, as if that alone would affect its meaningfulness and usefulness. In lieu of requiring only annual or biannual formal performance reviews—which many recognize as a colossal waste of time and effort—organizations have increased the cadence and number of performance feedback conversations with the expectation that that would bolster the performance management process as a whole. Stated simply, the assumption is that more feedback more often should yield stronger performance.

Performance management systems and platforms are now designed to track and document all of these conversations and not just formal reviews and agreements. Managers are now expected to improve feedback capacity as well as coaching capability in order to provide both more consistent and better feedback to employees. It makes sense logically, but in practice, it's a process that doesn't address relationships and the nature of how successful relationships really work.

> **Ideally, feedback conversations are meant to be meaningful and useful, not just frequent.**

Besides improved feedback and coaching, there is also increased pressure on management around employee engagement more broadly. Managers are measured by how well they manage people in maintaining the *brand*—a duty that is said to impact the company's ability to recruit top talent, reduce turnover, and retain high performers. In sum, companies have created a perfect storm for managers to fail at manager-employee relationships by way of continued poor communication.

Let's look at some of the research. In 2015, Lee Hecht Harrison did a study to specifically look at how companies were doing after setting the expectation of feedback and coaching, as well as providing formal training in coaching skills. Here's what they found:

Second only to lacking the proper skills for coaching, managers were not being held accountable for actually engaging in coaching conversations and activities. As if in response, the very next year, organizations invested even more effort in getting managers trained in the skills they needed to be good coaches. It is unclear which types of training they were offered, but the results suggest that managers were, at the very least, given additional tools for carrying out their responsibilities.

CHALLENGES FOR MANAGERIAL COACHING

LACK OF SKILLS, ACCOUNTABILITY, AND COMMITMENT ARE THE TOP CHALLENGES TO MANAGERIAL COACHING OF EMPLOYEES.

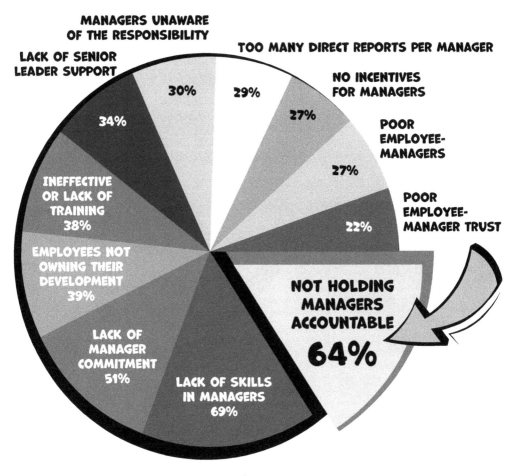

Figure 3

Then, in 2017, the International Coaching Federation (ICF)—an organization that has been monitoring the progress of the coaching industry since it was founded in 1995—conducted its own study to understand how organizations were implementing the practice.

Here's what the ICF study found:

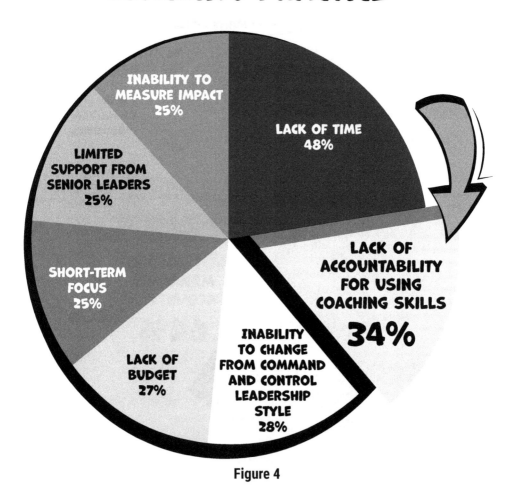

CHALLENGES FOR MANAGERIAL COACHING PRACTICE

INABILITY TO MEASURE IMPACT 25%

LIMITED SUPPORT FROM SENIOR LEADERS 25%

LACK OF TIME 48%

SHORT-TERM FOCUS 25%

LACK OF ACCOUNTABILITY FOR USING COACHING SKILLS

34%

LACK OF BUDGET 27%

INABILITY TO CHANGE FROM COMMAND AND CONTROL LEADERSHIP STYLE 28%

Figure 4

Notice in figure 4 above that nearly half the managers said they *lacked the time* to engage in coaching and that 34 percent said there was a *lack of accountability* for using the coaching skills to begin with.

I see time as a choice, as in: managers make choices about how they spend their time each day. Every choice made results in how managers ultimately perform. What the ICF report tells me is that managers are, in essence, choosing not to coach employees and are instead choosing to do something else they feel is more important. When you add in the absence of accountability, it seems reasonable that a manager might think, *I'm choosing not to spend time coaching, and there are no consequences for that. So I'm just taking that off my already full plate.* The bottom line is this: what these results all highlight is an accountability problem and not necessarily a coaching problem (though there may be problems with coaching too).

As a coach, I know the power of coaching as a means of driving change and improvement. I support the effort to include more coaching in organizations of all kinds. It's an absolutely fantastic idea that we instill this capability in our managers, and I believe that companies should be investing in it. But that's not the point.

My point here is this: If you want to get to all the results that coaching and development have to offer, you have to master accountability first.

I began this book with the assertion that holding someone to account is an act of clarity, so you might imagine that I feel compelled to create some clarity around the notions of *feedback* and *coaching*, especially insofar as they are unique from the practice of accountability. As organizations are working to embrace and invest in a *coaching culture* and are improving their knowledge base and coaching capability, some are already gaining clarity on the differences between these skill sets.

> **If you want to get to all the results that coaching and development have to offer, you have to master accountability first.**

I recognize that and apologize to those of you who feel I might be belaboring a point. For others, I suspect that my belaboring the point might help you get a grip on what you're actually trying to achieve.

Back in 2016, I stood up in front of a room of human resources practitioners who were attending an inaugural event centered on the much-needed makeover (or eradication) of performance management and performance review. I told the group that coaching and feedback are not the same thing and that anyone who continued to think of them as interchangeable terms and practices should immediately stop. The room went silent. I noted some furrowed brows and crossed arms, but I also saw some eyebrows raised in curiosity. I continued to pursue my point: feedback and coaching are related on a continuum; engaging in one can lead to the other. In this way, they're much like sitting and standing. You use the same muscle groups to do both, but for each, you're engaging those muscles in an entirely different activity.

Feedback is the primary communication skill used to achieve accountability. Accountability, however, demands more than just feedback. Think of it this way: managing performance as a whole is like setting the table for a conversation. The meal is called performance management. Accountability is what's on the menu. Feedback is like the plate. Coaching is dessert. So if we're talking about feedback, we're fundamentally talking about one among several performance management skills. Feedback is the unifying muscle group (your core) that can move you from sitting to standing, meaning it can move you from ownership of performance into development of performance. It's the lynchpin.

> **Feedback is the primary communication skill used to achieve accountability. Accountability, however, demands more than just feedback.**

Not until we get to the point of performance *development* does coaching come in. When done well, coaching is not just nudging, supporting, and problem solving performance issues. It's not just standing on the sideline and suggesting that someone else get out there and do a better job, either by explicitly telling that person what to do and how to do it or letting them figure it out on their own through trial and error. Instead, coaching involves a time commitment to teaching skills or aiding in behavior change that will help an employee become better at how they do what they do. Coaching, in other words, involves time spent practicing. Organizations struggle to build a *coaching culture* precisely because managers have repeatedly reported they "simply don't have time" for coaching, meaning they don't have time for practice. If they're getting paid for results and if they're being measured based on results, they're going to be focused on the *win*, and it will be *game time* all the time.

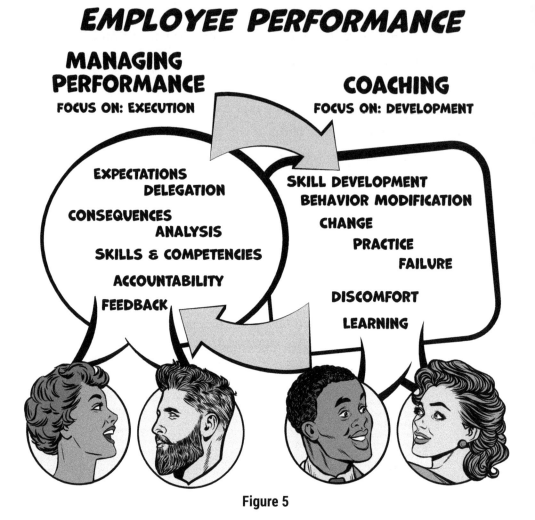

Figure 5

Full Accountability Has Three Key Parts

Full ownership—taking full responsibility for attitudes, behaviors, and work tasks—is the ultimate outcome that feedback, accountability, and coaching done right can offer, but they are distinct practices aimed at three unique types of ownership.

Accountability = Clarity and
CHOICE OWNERSHIP

Accountability begins with understanding what the issue is *for you* and analyzing where your employee or peer may have made a decision causing a poor result. First, *you* do the work, and then you verify your thinking in your conversation with that employee.

Feedback = Awareness and
PERFORMANCE OWNERSHIP

Feedback conversations are more than just an information dump, a time for you to get things off your chest or alert others to your disappointments. This aspect of accountability occurs when you share your perspective and experience and find out if the other person will take any ownership of that perspective. Only then can you move to the third aspect of accountability, which is the "now what?" part. If they'll own it, now what?

Coaching = Development and
CHANGE OWNERSHIP

Coaching may or may not be the next step. However, if you're going to do any kind of meaningful skill development or behavioral change work as a manager, coaching should always be considered as a next step. The central question of coaching is this: What does the person who's taken ownership do next to get better and to improve performance?

In both studies I mentioned earlier, the very reason managerial coaching was disappointing for organizations is not about *time*;

it's about not being held accountable for how their time was spent. The Lee Hecht Harrison recommendation was to "hold managers accountable," and the ICF study suggested to "hold all stakeholders accountable in a coaching culture."

And here's my point in sharing these with you: You cannot coach your way to better performance and higher engagement without addressing accountability first. Coaching, by its very nature, demands accountability skills even to have a chance at being effective.

If your organization, division, or team is going to be successful at developing people, building skills and capability, or changing behaviors, you cannot get there with feedback alone. You cannot get there with coaching alone. You must first build capability around accountability, then see what your coaching efforts bring to bear.

> You cannot coach your way to better performance and higher engagement without addressing accountability first.

When I train managers on accountability skills, one of the arguments with which I begin is this: *If you can own it, you can change it. If there's no ownership, there's no change.* If you're not working with the aim of achieving ownership from the get-go, you will not be able to achieve any real significant or sustainable form of performance improvement. Coaching always begins from a place of mutuality. You must have a willing participant in a coaching engagement, and that willingness comes from ownership of feedback and accountability. The same holds true of the accountability training process: when you focus first on and achieve a mindset and skill set for driving accountability, only then can you effectively activate your coaching capability to bring improvement and ultimately personal and professional growth—the mother lode of employee engagement.

The great news? *It's easier to hold people accountable than it is to coach their development.* Accountability takes practice, but not as much as you might think. Once you shift your mindset, it becomes much easier to do, and all your reservations and hesitations dissolve into an expression I hear regularly in every class I teach, even from the seasoned managers: "I wish I'd known this earlier in my career!"

You can effectively hold others accountable and achieve performance ownership, and when you do, you will improve your ability eventually to move into coaching and developing your employees, teams, and direct reports.

CHAPTER 4

The Accountability Mindset

ALL OF OUR CHOICES regarding how we behave ultimately derive from what we hold to be true—our beliefs—and what we deem to be important—our values. Most behavior change and skill development occur because we perceive value in those behaviors and skills. However, even if we believe that a behavior is important—for example, holding someone to account—we can develop a negative attitude around that belief if our experience attempting that behavior is consistently poor or difficult. My mindset around accountability is as much about how I myself engage in it, as well as how I've experienced it when others have held me accountable. In other words, our experiences form our mindset—for better or worse.

You can be at one end of the spectrum, where you believe that accountability is important (valuable), but your experience with it may not be positive and may be mostly fear-driven. Some of the people I've coached will tell me, "I'm conflict-averse" or "My top strength is harmony." What they are attempting to tell me is that they believe "I'm not good at" or "I don't like" holding people accountable. These people often manifest trepidation and uncertainty around accountability, making it difficult to act on it consistently or to any real impact. Many managers find themselves on this end of the spectrum, a condition I've named "fearful inconsistence"; at best, they'll experience difficulty and nervousness when it comes to having tough conversations, standing in the moment, creating clarity, and setting expectations.

At the other end of the spectrum, you'll find people whose frame of reference around accountability is tied to their sense of power. These managers will engage more consistently and more frequently, valuing short-term impact over long-term damage. These are people who make statements like "I've got no problem being honest; in fact, I'm probably too honest," which is often a couched version of "I'm blunt, and I don't care." They'll consistently overpower others, a condition I've named *consistent overpowering*, and they'll even act with malevolent intent. For them, humiliation is a fine enough tool for gaining compliance.

Both mindsets—on either end of this continuum—see accountability more as punitive than positive (see figure 6). The difference is that the people on the *fearful inconsistence* end of the spectrum find the idea of punishment painful, and the people on the *consistent overpowering* end of the spectrum take some pleasure in it. The further toward either extreme you are as a manager, the more your employees tend to perform either from malicious compliance or fundamental lack of clarity on what they are supposed to be doing. In neither case will managers gain true accountability.

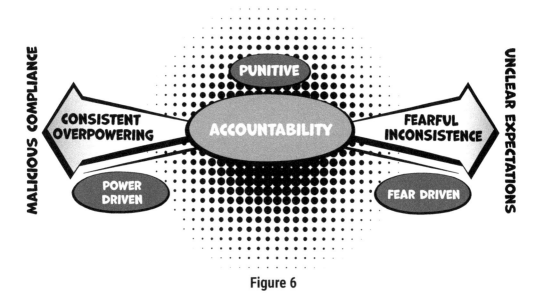

Figure 6

From Results First to Relationships First

A manager's mindset is a reflection of what that specific person holds to be important, which is often a reflection of what's reinforced within the organization as a cultural value. I mentioned in an earlier chapter the increased attention that's been given to employee engagement, to coaching, and to relationship building, but I want to point out that, alongside those concerns, we should recognize the attention paid to business results, deliverables, and measurables (widgets built and sold, client hours billed, packages delivered, patrons served) that are directly tied to revenue and profitability. As the saying goes, "what gets measured gets done," and since the *hard measures* I just named are the ones that are most likely to be central to a business enterprise, they tend to be what gets the most attention within organizational cultures.

EXPAND YOUR THINKING

GETTING TO "YES, AND..."

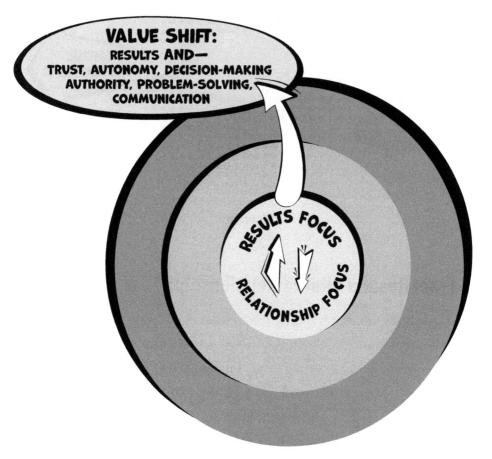

Figure 2

The irony of emphasizing the *hard measures* is that doing so contributes to a lack of accountability. Let me explain why. When results are the overriding driving force, they become the basis of how employee efforts are measured, rated, and rewarded. As a manager in a results-focused organization, I come to every conversation with results in mind. When I meet with my peers, when I meet with other divisions, when I meet with customers, when I meet with my direct reports, when I frame outcomes, when I write emails—whenever I engage—I motivate, see, hear, and feel all through a results-focused lens. Especially if I am ambitious, results come first.

Of course, it's completely normal that businesses emphasize results—results are what make the money that keeps a business viable and profitable! The thing is, that approach doesn't reflect how people are wired to be most productive, most innovative, and most willing to give discretionary effort. Focusing primarily on business results removes the personal connection and fails to leverage the power of the human effort. It may sound too ideal to say that to get the best advantage, we need to look at the human beings who work within a business as having more than just a superficial relationship. But this is not a mere ideal. It's also not new thinking. Those who work in human resources, organizational development, or other learning arms of their organizations know this already. They know that if the aim is to create a people-positive environment, to leverage human production, innovation, and willingness to go the extra mile on behalf of business results, then taking a *relationships-first* perspective is far and away more effective than a *results-first* approach. The problem comes in convincing some managers and leaders that this is the case.

Now, what if I told you that every manager actually makes a personal choice about which approach to take? Every manager decides her or his answer to the questions: What's more important to me? What do I hold to be true about delivering results for my organization? This choice stems from their fundamental beliefs about human nature as it does from the resulting organizational culture.

There are many managers who feel that they do not have that capacity to choose, who feel that their organizations regularly communicate to them, explicitly and implicitly, that they must select the results-first approach in order not to do damage to the company or even lose their jobs. You may even be thinking, *Relationships first sounds like a nice approach, but if I don't focus on results, they'll replace me with someone who will!* Or you may even be thinking, *A manager can get results either way, whether by focusing on results or relationships.*

Managing performance, especially driving accountability, is a relationship- and culture-forming skill set, a foundation-building capability. You've likely seen the difference between organizations and teams that do it and those that don't. And you well know that, as managers, you are the stewards of your culture. *You* are the person who ultimately decides how you approach accountability. My only argument here is that a people-first approach will serve you better. There's science behind that statement to back me up. Hop on Google and search "Robert Hartman and axiology," if you're inclined to learn more about the science of value. Bottom line: a people-first approach is scientifically proven to be of more value.

It's your employees' discretionary efforts that make the difference, and that's what makes employee engagement and relationship building so critical. If results come first for you, your ability to get any discretionary effort will be limited because you will have left it up to the individuals you are managing to be self-motivated and self-initiating of work. In fact, it's likely that you already do expect people to be intrinsically motivated and self-driven, most likely without having stated or clarified that expectation. In fact, you may even be someone who values self-motivation and self-initiation and feels, or takes for granted, that most others do too. But as you know, based on poor performance, not everyone does.

The truth is that even though self-motivation and initiative can be a shared value, it may not be a viable skill set for some of the people you manage. How many years now have we been *teaching to the test* in the United States, setting up our future workforce with a "just tell me what I need to know" expectation. Assuming self-motivation and independence can create a situation that damages work relationships, your feedback can sound to others like: *"I'm not sure what you're giving me here. This is not what I asked for. Go back and do it again, and do it better. Just figure it out."*

When you are results-driven and feel that it takes too much time to have a conversation involving context discovery and ownership, then you will continue to deliver at a mediocre level because you may just end up telling people what to do most of the time. However, when you value relationships first, when you put the people in front of the results, you'll be more driven to inquire about context instead of just making assumptions. You'll be more willing to make a small investment of time to have a clarifying conversation, knowing that it can yield compounded improvements. Doing that sounds to others more like: *"This isn't the kind of finished work I was expecting. It looks to me like you did not spend enough time really researching and then forming a complete design for a full campaign. Walk me through your process so I can help you pinpoint where you need improvement."*

Maybe you're someone who's somewhere in the middle of these two approaches—sometimes you're willing to make the time, and sometimes you feel you just don't have the time you believe it will take to dive into a conversation. This is where most managers find themselves. It's also why I talk about accountability conversations as a *practice* like yoga. Sometimes it takes intention to hold yourself in a place where you can be more effective. When you are able to practice the communications skills of accountability regularly, you will find that, in fact, it takes no more time to have a relationship-first conversation than it did to have a results-first conversation. In fact, as your team becomes accustomed to a relationship-first approach, your conversations may get even shorter than you might expect.

The relationship-first approach requires that you frame account-ability from a contextual standpoint and with a focus on gaining clarity. This approach puts emphasis on the dynamic in which you and the other person come together to discover where things stand (results status/impacts) and who owns what. That stands in sharp contrast to the results-first approach, which is an outward push to parse what went wrong and why we didn't get the outcome we wanted. The difference should be clear: A punitive mindset is focused on fault. A clarity mindset is focused on ownership.

From Someone Else's Responsibility to My Responsibility

When your team or employee has delivered a bad result, or when you've got an underperformer, whose issue is it? I often ask this question at the start of training sessions, and most of the time the resounding answer is: "It's theirs!" My response to this is: "No, it's not their issue. As the manager, it's *always* your issue first. It's your expectation, until the other person owns it." Being account-able is the ability to take ownership. When you have to hold someone accountable, the first question you must ask is: "What is *my* issue with this person and this situation? What are they doing or not doing that's not working for me?" The second question should always be: "Was I clear about my expectation?"

> A punitive mindset is focused on fault. A clarity mindset is focused on ownership.

Figure 7

When I drive accountability by putting relationships first, this means I must own my role in the relationship first. It's my job to set the expectation. It's my job to be clear about what I'm asking someone else to do and how I'd like it to be done (see figure 7). If I have a performance issue with someone, I basically am dealing with an unmet expectation of my own. *I have to be clear about what's going on for me, about the expectation I hold that's not being met.* I must be clear on this first, so I can then get clarity about what's going on with them. My aim here is to fully understand their underperformance.

> When you have to hold someone accountable, the first question you must ask is: "What is *my* issue with this person and this situation?

The bottom line is this: You must own your own issue first, if you expect to gain ownership from your direct reports, peers, or up-line managers. If you can't own your own issue, then you are just looking to distribute blame. The need to blame comes directly from shame about what *you* did or didn't do. And that need only fits with results-focused, depersonalized work. The need to blame is also how the "it's not my fault" train gets going. If we're not owning our own issues, we're setting ourselves up to be a victim of everyone else.

Your Mindset Matches Your Approach

Accountability applies in every direction. If you are aiming for a culture of accountability, that means you value and expect account-ability down-line, peer to peer, and up-line to leadership. Merely looking to have down-line accountability or down-line and peer-to-peer accountability without expecting feedback or questions pointed in your direction (and upward from there) is not accountability; that's hypocrisy, and everyone knows it.

When you have a culture of accountability, the overall mindset shift looks something like this:

Figure 8

Let's focus on each of the primary categories in turn.

Learning, Growth, and Change Focus

When you have an accountability mindset, you let go of trying to fix people by focusing on their deficits, skills gaps, and weaknesses, and you focus instead on learning and growth. We are already in an era

79

of strengths-based development. Think of having accountability conversations as an easy, everyday launching point for ongoing change and development. A relationship-first approach to performance, with its emphasis on ownership and trust, yields employees who are much more willing to change and challenge themselves.

> When you have an accountability mindset, you let go of trying to fix people by focusing on their deficits, skills gaps, and weaknesses, and you focus instead on learning and growth.

Critical Thinking and Cocreated Problem-Solving

Another shift in mindset comes from valuing discovery around the performance problems your employees or peers may have, as well as the discovery in how to solve problems together. The ability to ask questions that probe areas of concern as well as reveal how others think, make decisions, and approach their work is the heart of knowing and trusting others.

Reflective and Clear

Many managers, simply because they are experienced and want to solve problems quickly, make assumptions about why things are happening, about why decisions were made the way they were, and about the intentions or abilities of others. When you approach accountability from a place of clarity, you stop making assumptions. You reflect on your real expectations, and you inquire about what's actually driving your employees' behaviors.

Ownership and Solution Building

Moving from shame and blame to empowerment and ownership is the most freeing of the shifts that result from mastering accountability.

Shame and blame come from a place of fear. When you operate from that place, you limit solution building and genuine improvement.

Shame and blame are the most crippling states of mind to manage, yet so much of the time we place emphasis on shame and blame as if they were the only solutions to performance problems. But think about it: when we don't trust company leadership, or our peers, or other divisions or organizations, we operate from a place of self-protection. We shut off our ability to strategize effectively, to innovate and generate improvements and solutions that are long term, meaningful, and impactful for the business as a whole. Instead, we just move through crises, making choices focused around survival and delivering work products that are merely good enough.

By contrast, taking ownership situates us in a place of power—not power as total control but power understood as responsibility and as the ability to make decisions. We abdicate that true power all the time because we are unwilling to address either our own choices or the choices of others. We feel the pressure of responsibility for the choices made by those we manage. The power of ownership comes when you can easily and readily address your own choices as well as an employee's or teammate's choices without fear, anxiety, or drama.

Continuous and Daily Process

Accountability is a way of being, not a tool to leverage only in times of crisis. When we are accountable for all our choices, behaviors, and results, we become empowered human beings who are learning, changing, and growing together. This isn't to say there won't be ambitious, overstepping, micromanaging, and bad decision-making moments of failure. There will be. We're all still human. But continuous and daily practice to the contrary makes those instances far fewer and less damaging. In fact, if done right, continuous practice of accountability transforms those moments into opportunities for growth and change.

Intrinsic Motivation and Autonomy

If we are faced with no choice, little room for real decision-making, and no trust from our senior managers and leaders, we invest little and strive only for compliance. When our team is merely a source of complaining and venting, Facebook and the internet will seem far more interesting than the work we've been asked to do.

To the contrary, when meaningful and useful feedback is provided, when accountability is present and the norm, that clarity makes room in our thinking for better decision-making and greater understanding about how we can add value to our own work. Accountability, in other words, is what fires our intrinsic motivation. When we are clear about our level of decision-making and our impact, and when we cultivate trust through a relationship-first approach, we achieve a sense of autonomy and purpose. We feel connected to our work and our team.

Engagement

Engagement can be powerful. In Gallup's Seven Stages of the Employee Journey, engagement is one of the three stages in which most employees spend time with your organization-building strengths and purpose.[10] Clarity and trust around strength, purpose, expectation, and improvement deliver discretionary effort in a way that no punitive measures can achieve.

---

10   Ryan Pendell, "Employee Experience vs. Engagement: What's the Difference?" Gallup Workplace, October 12, 2018, https://www.gallup.com/workplace/243578/employee-experience-engagement-difference.aspx.

Practice Builds Muscle Memory

Our management capabilities are very much a product of what we've learned by being managed. And our management communication is very much a product of our personal style and experience of organizational pressures and norms.

Some managers and leaders are already excellent communicators and just need to reframe how they think about the accountability conversation. They can achieve radically improved results around accountability and performance in a very short period—sometimes days or weeks. Other managers and leaders are not as polished or confident and need more time to reframe how they understand accountability conversations and to practice and apply a new way of addressing them.

A manager's ability to take ownership for their own beliefs and actions around accountability directly impacts their ability to take on better, more advanced communication skills, as well as their willingness to practice and apply those skills. Using a skill set that sets up the conversation for critical thinking and problem-solving can change the attitude, the beliefs, and even the neurochemistry of people who choose to stand in the moment of accountability. Daily effort and practice are important parts of that transformation. If we don't make shifting our mindsets part of that practice, we're likely to default to old behavioral tendencies when we're operating at speed and under pressure. The trick is to replace those old default practices—the behavioral tendencies we've leaned on or cultivated over our lifetimes—with new and more productive ones.

CHAPTER 5

Your Brain on Accountability

WE SEE AND EXPERIENCE the world through sensation or feeling, and we understand and connect to each other about those feelings through our words. When I was a theater director, part of my work process involved going through a script, line by line, and assigning each line of dialogue an active verb meant to describe the *want* or *need* of that line. The dialogue of a play is broken down into points of emphasis (like musical beats) that drive the rhythm or energy of a scene. That exercise was a way of beginning to understand and see the verbal score (just like a musical score) of the play. Of course, that process was driven by my interpretation of the language—how I read it, felt it, heard it—which ultimately provided the basis for how I directed it.

Ultimately, as you well know, it's not just my interpretation of the words that matters. The actors bring their energy and perspective to the roles, and it's the collaborative effort among us that ultimately determines how the lines are delivered. Next, add in the audience to that experience. How each person in that audience hears and responds is also part of the connections made by every theatrical event. We all started out with the same words provided by the playwright. The language is always the basis of the experience, but each performance is still unique.

The same is true for workplace accountability. It both starts and ends with the language. Of course, those real-world conversations are improvisational, meaning you interpret language in the moment—you read it, feel it, hear it—and you respond based on that awareness. Communicating in conversation with someone is more complex than we tend to acknowledge because it's not just about the content or message. It's also about how we feel about what we hear, what our experience is, and how we feel about that experience as it is happening. All of that goes into our process of making sense to, and of, one another. That's why I insist that:

Our conversations ARE our relationships.
Our relationships ARE our culture.

How we talk to someone—our tone of voice, level of intensity (pitch, speed, volume), the frequency in which we speak to them, and the language we choose—determines the kind of relationship we are having. Conversely, if we are not speaking to someone, we are not having a relationship with them. If we are only speaking through text or through email, we are *barely* having a relationship, and more likely than not it's one filled with assumptions and *realities* of our own making. That's because our brains will fill in the gaps for all that's missing—all the communication that happens via nonverbal signals.

Along these same lines, the conversations we have most of the time are what build the organization's culture. So if 90 percent of an organization's conversations happen via email, what does that tell you about what's important culturally in that organization? It's placing information over people a full 90 percent of the time.

Now, imagine a conversation with an underperforming or struggling employee. In some critical way, she or he is not meeting expectations, and that is having a negative impact on you personally, as well as on the business. In other words, imagine that the stakes of this conversation are high. The common reaction to this scenario is "Yeah, that's why accountability is so hard!" to which I say, "Yes. And no." Yes, you need all your skills to be activated, to have all your players on the field, so to speak. You need your language, your eyeballs, your para-linguistics (breathing, articulation, tone, pitch, intonation, speed), and your body language to be effective and fully present in the game. But once you have skills in these areas and understand how to utilize them, accountability conversations are not so hard at all to do well.

What you absolutely shouldn't do with your underperforming employee is just email or text that employee to tell them that they're underperforming and to provide constructive feedback. Emails and texts are *only* words—only one part of communication. In an email or text, you're leaving the bulk of your message up to your reader to interpret or fill in, based on their experience of you, how they feel about you, and their relationship with you. Even if you feel you've got a great relationship with someone, by using email or text as a substitute for what should be a face-to-face conversation, or at a minimum a web-based and cameras-on exchange, you're still allowing a huge gap for misinterpretation, assumptions, and the stories we tell ourselves. And *no*, emojis, gifs, avatars, and effects do not make up for the missing context.

A conversation about clarity and ownership requires live dialogue and full presence. Even if someone only verbalizes "I got it," you can notice what else they might be saying nonverbally. And when you consider that language may betray the real message, that your employees may choose to use the language they believe their managers want to hear, you can see that you'll need to uncover the messages that are hiding behind or alongside the words that are used.

Changing Your Language Changes Minds

In my thirty-plus years in coaching, and in training and development, communication skills have always been *the number one skill set* requested by clients and most needed by executives, managers, and leaders at any level. In a growing business culture centered around teams, soft skills are even more important.

There is hard science behind arguments for soft skills like accountability. In 2018, I began studying and working with Judith E. Glaser, author of *Conversational Intelligence*, or what she calls C-IQ, to become certified in her theories and methods.[11] Glaser's work provides excellent context for understanding why communication skills are so critical for business. If you're not already familiar with her work, let me give you a quick tutorial on three main concept areas that can help us make sense of accountability conversations and show what neuroscience and neurochemistry tell us about language, as well as how our biology backs up the need to master communication.[12]

The foundation of any good relationship is trust. Trust happens much faster in person, and that's because of the role played by our limbic systems and our brains. The three key concepts that I take from Glaser for establishing trust and mastering accountability are:

1. Connectivity

2. Feel good/feel bad conversations

3. Regulating the neurochemical state of mind

---

11 *All or parts of the content presented here are adapted from* Conversational Intelligence *and the work of Judith E. Glaser.*

12 If you'd like to go deeper, here's the current link to Dr. Lieberman's TED Talk: https://www.youtube.com/watch?v=NNhk3owF7RQ.

Connectivity

In order to dip into the lessons from neurochemistry, we have to look first at Maslow's hierarchy of needs. You're probably familiar with Maslow's pyramid.

Abraham Maslow proposed this hierarchy in his 1943 paper "A Theory of Human Motivation" in *Psychological Review*. The model is often described as follows:

> The most fundamental and basic four layers of the pyramid contain what Maslow called "deficiency needs" or "d-needs": esteem, friendship and love, security, and physical needs. If these "deficiency needs" are not met—with the exception of the most fundamental (physiological) need—there may not be a physical indication, but the individual will feel anxious and tense. Maslow's theory suggests that the most basic level of needs must be met before the individual will strongly desire (or focus motivation upon) the secondary or higher-level needs. Maslow also coined the term "metamotivation" to describe the motivation of people who go beyond the scope of the basic needs and strive for constant betterment.[13]

Essentially, Maslow theorized that our primary needs are physical, followed by emotional needs around belonging, followed by intellectual needs around actualization.

The science of neurochemistry has come to question Maslow's assertion, based on recent discoveries in how our brains are wired. What neuroscientists like Matt Lieberman are now learning is that our need to connect is much stronger than our need for personal safety.[14]

---

13   Frank G. Goble, *The Third Force: The Psychology of Abraham Maslow* (Richmond, CA: Maurice Bassett Publishing, 1970), 62.

14   Matthew D. Lieberman, *Social: Why Our Brains Are Wired to Connect* (New York: Crown, 2013).

MASLOW'S HIERARCHY OF NEEDS

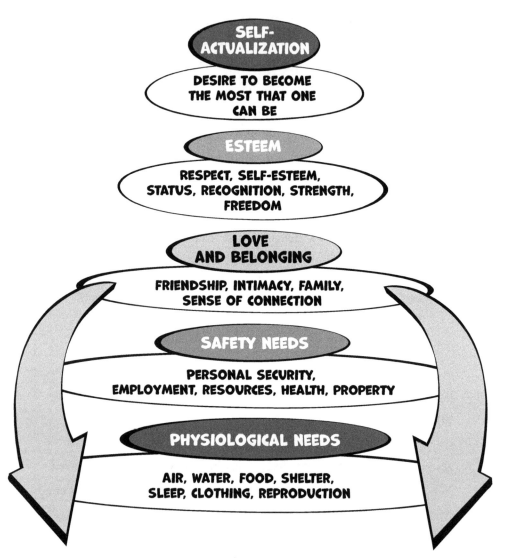

Figure 9

This, of course, explains all our behaviors in junior high and high school, right? Think about some of your decisions back then and the difference between your concern for personal safety versus hanging out with the cool kids, just sayin'. This also explains the pandemic surges that followed upon the 2020 holidays. Many people were more than willing to sacrifice their personal safety to feel connected to others. Connecting to others at work, at home, and socially is essential to our very survival as human beings. It's an emotional drive.

From my perspective, and certainly from Judith E. Glaser's, the need for human connection explains so much about miscommunication. On the one hand, miscommunication can stem from a lack of empathy, where we don't feel connected to the other person, or we don't share the urgency, perspective, or experience of the other person, and judge them accordingly. On the other hand, miscommunication can stem from misreading someone's intentions, as when we interpret their meaning differently from how they may have intended it—a missed (or botched) connection if ever there was one.

All conversations are attempts at connection. How well are we connecting when we hold others accountable?

Feel Good/Feel Bad Conversations

Our brain chemistry helps to explain why we hold on to things people said that are negative and why, oppositely, certain conversations make us feel great.

As we communicate, we trigger a neurochemical cocktail that makes us feel either good or bad; the *good* cocktail is primarily a mix of dopamine, oxytocin, and serotonin, and the *bad* cocktail is primarily a mix of cortisol, norepinephrine, and testosterone. In communication, we translate those good or bad feelings into words, sentences, and stories. This is where the "ladder of inference" concept comes from. Originated in 1970 by Chris Argyris, a Harvard Business School professor, the ladder of inference describes the mental process by which we draw conclusions about experiences and events.[15] Judith E. Glaser refers to the laddering phenomenon as the "ladder of conclusions." It begins with a bioreaction, followed by a feeling, then a thought (at which point we begin to attach language), then a belief (based on how we've named and framed the thought), and finally a conclusion where we have assigned and connected assumptions, interpretations, and meaning. This laddering process unleashes a neurochemical reaction, which is essentially a mix of hormones that are directly associated with our assumptions, interpretations, and meaning. According to Glaser's work, as well as research of other neuroscientists she's studied, this whole laddering phenomenon takes place in about 0.07 seconds.

The net effect of the laddering process is that we essentially make up a story—either a good story or a bad story. Good stories release mostly dopamine, oxytocin, and serotonin, and bad stories release mostly norepinephrine, testosterone, and cortisol. This is why we feel a certain way based on the kind of conversation we're having. *Feel good* conversations trigger higher levels of dopamine, oxytocin, endorphins, and other chemicals that give us a sense of well-being.

The millions of minute-by-minute neurochemical reactions within our brains drive our states of mind. These states of mind affect the way we attempt to build trusting relationships with others, how we communicate, and how we shape our relationships. When we anticipate that conversations meant to hold people to account will be negative, we put ourselves in a place of increased cortisol, triggering our own *feel bad* state of mind. That negative thinking calls up in us a *fight and protect* neurochemical response—one which distances us from our ability to be strategic, to access our insight, and to fully see options for mutual success going forward.

---

15   You can learn more about the ladder of inference here: https://www.pon.harvard.
edu/tag/ladder-of-inference/.

The simple science is this: we don't operate our brains as a whole. We activate specific areas of our brains at any given time. When we are in *fight and protect* mode, our amygdala is activated. The amygdala is a collection of cells near the base or back of the brain—the *oldest* part of the brain—that governs our sense of physical and emotional safety, which I'll also refer to as our "lizard brain." Oppositely, when we are in collaboration and cocreating with others, we've activated our prefrontal cortex, or the front part of our brain, which is active in decision-making and in moderating social behavior.

What I've learned from Glaser is that we cannot operate from our amygdala (lizard brain/back of our head) and our prefrontal cortex (executive brain, strategy, insight, wisdom/front of our head) at the same time. *We can move from one to the other quite easily, but we cannot operate from both at once.* So a negative perspective creates negative chemistry, which then inhibits our capacity for strategizing and reinforces poor focus and less-than-stellar problem-solving. Scientifically speaking, this is why either speaking to your employee when you're in *fight or protect* mode or having your employee respond out of anger, disappointment, and frustration delivers less-than-desirable outcomes in these conversations.

Another way of looking at this neurochemical dynamic is to understand it as a *trust/no trust* dynamic (see figure 10). When we are operating from our amygdala/back of our head, in a cortisol-based cocktail, we are in a place of *no trust*. We neither trust nor feel safe, so we operate from a mindset of *fight and protect*—we put up our defenses. Have you ever had the experience of asking one of your staff or team members the status of a project or deliverable only to find that they respond to you defensively? That is what Glaser calls an "amygdala hijack," when people move to a state of defensiveness with seemingly no provocation.[16] The neurology of this is simple. The staff member or teammate felt the pressure of the question, and in an effort to identify the feeling, the brain turned to past experience; prior experience looked for language to deal with the feeling, and the brain came to a conclusion as a way of finding safety. That whole process happened in less than a second. And that reaction—which takes no effort and no time at all to achieve—is exactly why some of us do not want to have accountability conversations. We fear precisely this reaction. And it does happen. It *will* happen to you.

The good news is that we have some control over this. We have control in the form of language—both the language we use internally (our self-talk) and the language we use to do what I call "setting the table," which is the act of placing a performance issue on the table and inviting ownership. We have control because we recognize the need to change another person's neurochemical state for the better.

What it means to prepare for an accountability conversation is to choose the language that best represents, for you, the issue you are having and how it's impacting you, your team or your area of responsibility, the business—or all of those things. The need to guard against a response that's been subject to an amygdala or "lizard brain" hijack necessitates that the language you choose is specific and concise. You need to give the clearest indications possible of precisely what's going on. This is why speaking off the cuff or in the moment—doing no preparation or just speaking and then reacting—can be extremely counterproductive. A person's experience and perspective of you can change in a single conversation, especially a high-stakes conversation.

---

16   Judith E. Glaser, *Conversational Intelligence: How Great Leaders Build Trust and Get Extraordinary Results* (Routledge, 2014).

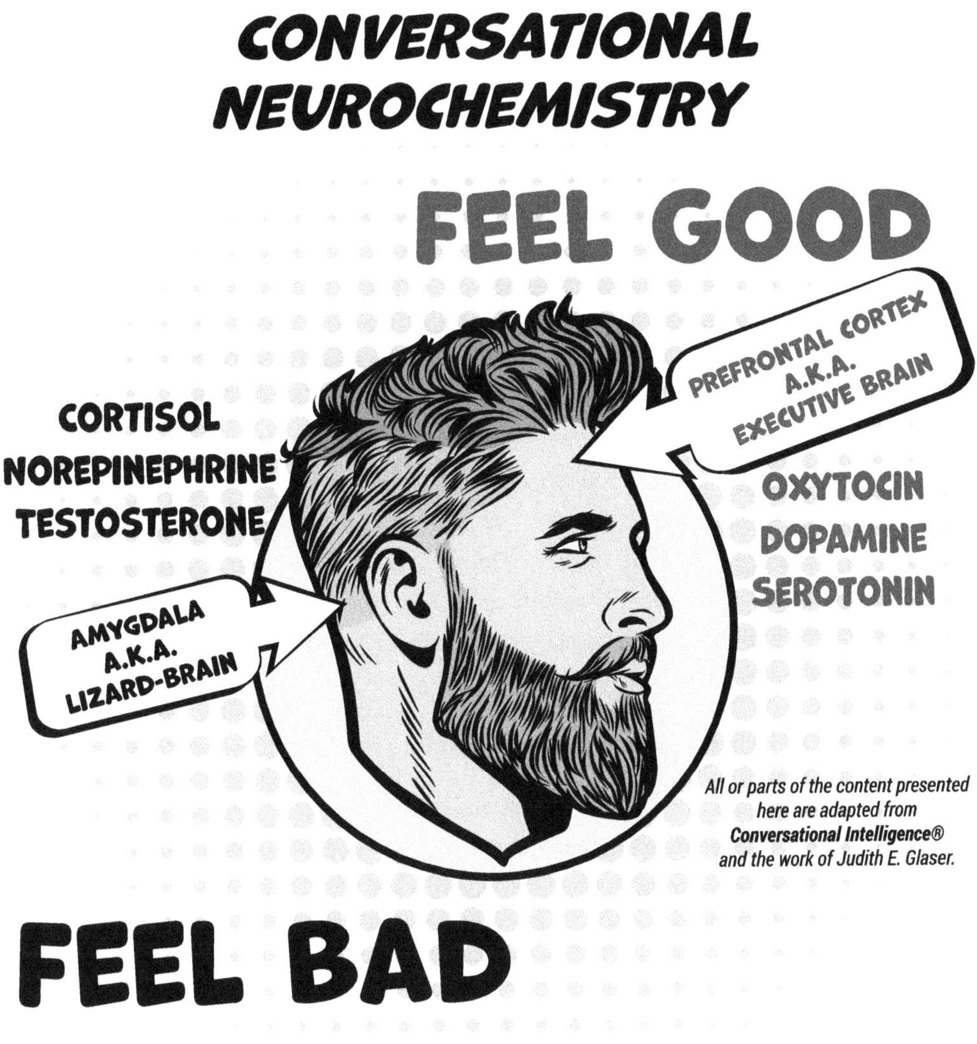

Figure 10

When you don't stop to think a little deeper about your issue, you can end up communicating many things that muddy, or make confusing, what ought to be clear. You can end up talking around an issue or even misidentifying it. To be good at accountability conversations—to be a better manager and leader—you must work on your ability *to reflect before you speak.* And that means being honest with yourself about what's really at issue.

That can be harder work than it seems. I've noticed that when managers begin to state their issues, they'll offer a backstory about context and results that may not really represent the primary issue. Here's an example of how that first attempt might sound:

> *"Juan, thanks for coming in to meet with me. I wanted to let you know I really appreciate all the work you're doing, and I know you're really working to pitch in for the team while we've been understaffed. But I'm worried about the time you're coming in. Is there something going on, or is there something we can do to make sure you get here on time? Your lateness is becoming a problem for others on the team, and we really need to be sure everyone is here on time. It's important for the team that everyone is here at the start of the day. Is there anything I can do to help?"*

Or that first attempt might sound like this:

> *"Tasha, you're one of the best producers on the team. Your work has always been top notch. However, you seem to be getting final drafts of our monthly reports turned in late. I know the process is difficult, and getting input from the other divisions can be problematic. This has been happening for a little while now, and so I'm a little concerned. Is there a problem I can help you with? Is there something I can do to help you get things back on track?"*

In both cases, there's a willingness to engage the other person, but the language is fraught with uncertainty and lack of clarity. If I'm the manager who said it, I'm putting a lot on the table and delivering a mixed message. In the attempt to talk with Juan, the manager has minimized the issue, almost to the point of making it a nonissue by softening and couching it within a litany of reasons as to why it's not really important. In the latter case, with Tasha, the manager is essentially making the following points: you're great; your work is late; the process is terrible; what can *I* do? If you stand back from either message to look at them through a theater director's eyes, you'll have a hard time trying to assign an active verb to either one. You'll have a hard time, in other words, determining the answer to the question "What does that manager want?" from the words that manager has said. Is the emphasis on the lateness? Is it on the process? Is it about being worried? Or is the manager just looking for ways to help?

Later on, we'll consider better versions of these attempts to name the issue. For now, let's focus on looking at them from the neurochemical standpoint that I've been emphasizing here. In particular, let's focus on what's happening for Tasha, the underperformer and object of the second message. She may have come to the conversation in full trust, but depending on her relationship with her manager, Tasha is probably showing up in a state of what's called *conditional trust* (see figure 11). Judith E. Glaser describes conditional trust as a state of trust in which we're willing but wary. We're trying to make sense and meaning of what we're experiencing as well as look for recognizable patterns of communication and seek a sense of belonging. When the manager speaks the words about getting reports in late, that's when Tasha's amygdala is most likely to be hijacked and when she's most likely to go into fight and protect mode. Given that the manager has couched the problem in acknowledgment of the difficult process, Tasha has also been provided with the exact reason she can use *to disown* her performance results.

Ultimately, Tasha is likely to walk away feeling badly and somewhat concerned but also justified in her performance. Her manager is likely to walk away feeling better that she's managed to bring the problem to Tasha's attention and most likely to assume that Tasha now understands she's got to do better. The reality of the situation? Nothing is likely to change, especially not in a long-term or permanent way, because ownership of the issue was never really sought by the manager.

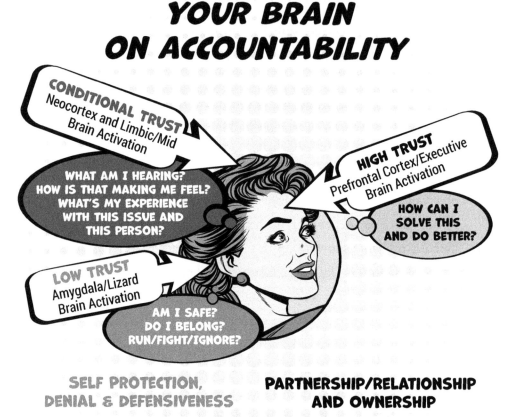

YOUR BRAIN ON ACCOUNTABILITY

CONDITIONAL TRUST
Neocortex and Limbic/Mid Brain Activation

WHAT AM I HEARING?
HOW IS THAT MAKING ME FEEL?
WHAT'S MY EXPERIENCE
WITH THIS ISSUE AND
THIS PERSON?

HIGH TRUST
Prefrontal Cortex/Executive Brain Activation

HOW CAN I
SOLVE THIS
AND DO BETTER?

LOW TRUST
Amygdala/Lizard Brain Activation

AM I SAFE?
DO I BELONG?
RUN/FIGHT/IGNORE?

SELF PROTECTION,
DENIAL & DEFENSIVENESS

PARTNERSHIP/RELATIONSHIP
AND OWNERSHIP

All or parts of the content presented here are adapted from **Conversational Intelligence**® and the work of Judith E. Glaser.

Figure 11

To be more effective, to get ownership and change, we've got to change the management approach out of the gate by considering how our language is likely to impact another person. We've also got to consider our own mindset and how our own anticipation regarding the other person affects us. Depending on how we're situated, that mindset can offer us an advantage or set us up with a disadvantage from the start.

If we're holding on to our fears about accountability and thinking that accountability means conflict, then we're already at a disadvantage neurochemically—we're already operating from a place of high cortisol and distrust. In that state, inquiring about performance results is going to seem like the opposite of ownership. It's going to seem

> To be more effective, to get ownership and change, we've got to change the management approach out of the gate by considering how our language is likely to impact another person.

more like lobbing a turd over the fence with the question in our minds: Are they gonna pick it up and deal with it, or are they gonna throw that shit back?

Regulating the Neurochemical State of Mind

The third relevant concept from C-IQ is called regulating. Within the context of a conversation, you and the other person will both be moving through your brain's neurochemical responses based on the specifics of the exchange—the words spoken, how they're spoken, the body language, and all the other paralinguistic signals your brains pick up. The exchange will either upregulate you (move you toward your prefrontal cortex, *executive brain*, toward strategy, insight, and wisdom) or downregulate you (move you toward your amygdala, into fight and protect mode), or hopefully get you to a place of what's called *coregulating* (where both of you are in a state of trust or conditional trust), which is the goal for the best, most productive conversations.

Coregulating exchanges offer the opportunity to cocreate solutions and achieve mutual gain.

Here's the most important thing to remember: the entire act of neurochemical regulation is driven by language, by *what* you actually say and *how* you say it, both verbal and nonverbal. That's why your preparation for a conversation about accountability is extremely important. You need to think about what you want to say, specifically. If you just speak off the cuff, your chances of coregulating are vastly diminished.

If you're someone who's been managing people for a long time, you may think that your situation is different. But what I've noticed is that people who have been managing others for a long time spend *even less time* thinking about their approach to a conversation from a language standpoint. Instead, they tend to think about the outcome they want and focus only on the result. Quite frankly, executives are notorious for speaking off the cuff, *precisely because* they've been managing for a long time and feel that their communication must be effective. Because executives are in the habit of relying on existing communication patterns, they're not thinking about preparation at this level. The thing is, accountability conversations demand a conscious effort around language, precisely because these are conversations aimed at clarity.

When I teach managers how to put an issue on the table, how to give feedback or confront performance issues that have been ongoing regardless of feedback, I work specifically on the language of the conversations they intend to have. I know that their ability to upregulate and coregulate will determine their success in garnering ownership, in arriving at real solutions, and ultimately in consistently achieving accountability. Consistent ownership is the cultural standard that will shift organizational performance.

Lack of trust is probably the number one reason for employee disengagement from management and from an organization more broadly. The specific by-product of coregulating is building trust, living in trust, and maintaining trust. Every accountability conversation is an opportunity to build trust and thereby build relationships through clarity and ownership. Account-ability conversations clarify what part each person plays to create success. Building trust through language builds the confidence that reinforces relationships and individuals' parts in them.

> **Consistent ownership is the cultural standard that will shift organizational performance.**

The results?

We feel connected and safe. Our primary needs are met, and we can better engage in rational reflection.

PART II
Skill Shift

EXPAND YOUR THINKING
GETTING TO "YES, AND..."

Figure 12

MINDSET AND PRACTICE are not mutually exclusive. Each directly impacts the other. If you recall my point from an earlier chapter: you need to shift your mindset to shift your experience, and you need to shift your experience to shift your mindset.

Think about it like this: our willingness to try something new is predicated on how we think about it. We can increase both our confidence about our ability to do something new depending on the words we use to talk about it and our ability to see or imagine ourselves doing it. Imagining what it would be like precedes trying that new thing.

That cycle of moving between mindset and practice is how we change over time to become someone who thinks different thoughts and takes different actions than the person we were before. It's also why actors always ask, "What's my motivation?" about the characters they're playing. They're asking, "How am I thinking about this internally?" so that they can generate a behavior to match. Are they motivated by the need to look good all the time? Are they motivated by the need to act courageously? Or the need to always please others? The behaviors will be different, depending on the answer.

In the chapters that follow, we'll begin looking at how to change our experience of accountability not just by thinking differently but also by *doing* differently. Not until both work in unison can we establish accountability as part of organizational culture and as a way of life.

We've so far reviewed what's at stake in shifting our values—the identification of what's most important so as to put relationships before results—and we've been examining accountability in context—how it's used, how it's experienced, and how it should be approached to be easier and more effective. If you're convinced about the need for the specific mindset shifts we've reviewed so far, you're likely ready to move on to our next point of focus—shifting our skills—through the actual practice or *performance* of the steps I'll lay out here.

A skills shift requires focusing not just on the *what* of accountability but also on the *how*. Expectations, tasks, and results are the *what*. These receive the most attention because success in work is usually measured by determining whether you delivered *what* was asked of you. Many managers believe they're very good at setting expectations. However, when they look carefully at how that's happening, their opinions of themselves often change. That's especially true for managers who've been doing a job for a long time. Their skills have become such strong muscle memory for them that they just roll with what they know. They have become what is called "unconsciously competent," meaning they no longer know what they know; they just do it. They tend to have feelings of satisfaction and complacency around the skill or behavior they're currently utilizing.

When you practice accountability, you'll need to become what is called "consciously competent," meaning you are aware of which skills you've mastered and which you haven't and can be fully present when practicing accountability so that you can become better at it. To be consciously competent is to become more of a critical thinker in the moment. That act of critical thinking in the moment is what facilitates a shift to focusing on *how* and not just *what*.

Now, let's get to broadening your knowledge about the *how* with my model of *how to do* accountability.

Six Ownership Steps of Accountability: The S.O.S. Conversation Model

The practice of workplace accountability is a six-step process and at most a five-minute conversation. This is what I call the S.O.S. Conversation. S.O.S. stands for Six Ownership Steps. The conversation itself can be shorter or longer depending on situational complexities and your specific performance of it. Once you've got the six steps down, you can have an accountability conversation in the hallway in two minutes. However, you'll never get there if you don't invest in practicing the conversation model every chance you get. And remember, it's a conversation. That means you should be expecting to receive a response and to engage in a dialogue.

It's very tempting to intellectualize the model and think, *Well, that's easy. I've got it, thanks, and I'm off to go do it.* For a rare few, that may be true. However, I can tell you that although it gets easy after intentional practice, it is not as easy as it looks when you first try it out. That's essentially why I've asked you to think about the practice of accountability conversations as being like the practice of yoga. You're not just doing the conversational version of a beginner-level Warrior Pose. You're doing the conversational version of One-Handed Tree Pose; if you're familiar with the pose, you'll recognize the sort of challenge I'm talking about. You're going to need some *muscle memory* to get you there confidently and consistently, and you have to engage your practice every day. You're always working to engage your whole self—your mind, your emotions, your body. When you are a master of accountability, you can be fully in the conversation—mentally, emotionally, and physically. That means you've thought about the conversation and strategized your approach; you are aware of and can adapt emotionally to ensure you don't tap out in the middle of the conversation; and, physically, you are focused, you make eye contact and stay calm, and all your nonverbal communications are nonthreatening and nonjudgmental. That's the goal.

Figure 13

The model you see here illustrates the accountability experience. I've designed it to help you see how to engage in the whole event from start to finish. You can see by looking at the illustration that an accountability conversation relies on more than just good feedback skills. It's about how you prepare, engage, and then close out. You'll notice, too, that clarity about who owns what is *one* important piece that follows from how you think about accountability at the outset and how you determine precisely what is unclear. Beyond the point of arriving at clarity, the accountability conversation also involves owning the next steps to rectify what's not working. In other words, there's more to the model than just the moment of the conversation itself (which is where the feedback happens). The whole experience is an arc—the shift from unclear to clear to "now, what?"—from issue, to ownership, to change. I'll share with you the best skills to employ at each stage, so you can see where *you* may need to work more.

CHAPTER 6

Step 1: Identify Your Issue

Figure 14

THE FIRST THING YOU DO when you drive accountability is determine what the issue is—for you. If you expect to get anyone to take ownership of a performance issue, you have to own what the issue is in the first place. Remember, it's your issue until the person with whom you're having the issue takes ownership of it.

Don't Confuse Issues with Results

Say you have a staff member who is sloppy with their work; it's hurried and they don't review it or think it through before handing it off. It's poorly presented, and it contains mistakes. What's the issue? Is sloppiness the issue? Or is it professionalism? Is it personal integrity around work product? Are they underestimating how much time they need to complete the work at a higher standard? Do they procrastinate? Are there clear product standards? Do they have the right experience with tools or platforms?

From your perspective, what's really going on?

When you take a moment to reflect and ask yourself deeper questions about a poor result, you'll get closer to the crux of your issue. Have you been explicit in setting the expectation? Have they been trained? Have they performed this task and delivered a better result previously? Do you see a behavior pattern that's new or different than what you've seen or experienced in the past? What about this outcome or result is not okay for you? What are the important aspects of this task/outcome that are coming in under par?

You might begin by guessing that the issue is sloppy work but then come around to identifying a new behavior pattern of lower attention to detail and investment in the work itself.

Given that you're doing some speculating and sleuthing at this point—after all, you have yet to talk with this employee—why is this step so important? Imagine starting the conversation talking about sloppy work. The individual may just say to you in response, "Yeah, I know. I need to get it together. I'll do better next time." Sloppiness is easy enough to correct, but it may not be the real driver behind what's happening. Now imagine starting the conversation with "You know I have expectations regarding the high standard around the quality of work on this project. I'm concerned because the quality of your work has gone down recently, and that's creating more rework and generating concern and frustration for others on the project. How do you see it?" This way of framing the issue—or setting the table—demands more engagement and deeper reflection from the other person. It creates space for the person to think about *how* they are working, not just *what* was wrong about what they did.

Reflect, Don't React

The key is to create space in your own thinking. You can do that by identifying any false assumptions you might be making and by ensuring that you are not merely reacting to a disappointment. When you react in the moment—say you shoot off an email with curt comments or statements—or when you move quickly into behavior that demonstrates shaming and blaming, you have not taken the time to reflect. You are working from your "lizard brain," that "amygdala hijack" I mentioned in chapter 5, and not operating strategically within your prefrontal cortex. Without reflecting, you cannot initiate conversation that utilizes your insight and wisdom, and you won't be open to what the other person has to say in response. Without reflecting, you are judging and rejecting—two relationship killers and trust breakers. *Relationship first* is also *reflection first*, not reaction.

Once you've opened yourself to reflecting instead of reacting, you'll be more likely to do the same with the other person. I asked a room full of experienced managers to think about a performance conversation, someone they know who needs feedback to improve performance in some way, and to demonstrate how they would begin that conversation. A brave volunteer started us off. She began like this: "Hi. I wanted to talk to you about your time management skills. I think you need to look at how you're spending your time, because

I don't feel you are getting back with customers in a period of time that works for them."

Not a bad start—not terrible, but not as accurate as she could be. I asked her, "What is your expectation regarding the amount of time that's acceptable for getting back to a customer?"

She said, "Well, it depends on what the service is, but I would expect a return call on resolution or status within twenty-four hours."

I asked her, "Are customers promised this? Do they expect to hear back in twenty-four hours?"

"Yes," she said.

I suggested, "Then why don't you use that?"

Her eyebrows went up. "How do you mean?" she inquired.

Think about it. If your issue is that your employee doesn't return calls or get back to customers within twenty-four hours, just state that. Why make it a bigger, less clear issue by calling it "time management"? When you start with "time management," who knows what you're ultimately going to be talking about? That conversation could go a million ways, and you've got no real sense of how it might turn out. So talk about the expectation. Doing so would sound more like this: "Hi, I wanted to talk to you about your twenty-four-hour customer contact time. You aren't making this consistently with customers. Talk to me about that." Straight to the point. Here's what's happening. Tell me more. The most important thing about getting straight to the point is that you avoid talking about a host of things you don't really need to talk about when you invite them into the conversation. The result? You're going to understand much better what they'll own and what they won't.

The first rule of accountability is this: If they can own it, they can change it. If they won't own it, they won't change it. But you need to be clear on what "it" is, and don't beat around the bush trying to express it. Don't overgeneralize, don't couch, don't cushion, and don't be afraid to state it clearly and concisely.

Clarity in the way you state your issues is how you set the table for the conversation to happen. Your clarity and your interest in the other person's reply are indicated by the words you choose, your tone of voice, and your capacity to refrain from judgment.

Now imagine if I were to change the previous example just slightly to say: "Hey listen, we've got a problem with your customer contact time. You're not getting back with them in twenty-four hours, so you need to pick up

> **The first rule of accountability is this: If they can own it, they can change it. If they won't own it, they won't change it.**

your game and pay more attention to what you're working on. Maybe you need to think about how you're managing your time."

I'm saying essentially the same thing, but with this approach, I've already decided what the problem is and how to fix it. I'm essentially just letting them know. I've also made no room for ownership. Just because they heard me and now know about my issue does not mean they'll own it or do anything to change it. I've just said it out loud and probably made them feel badly in the process.

Here are a few additional examples of how to begin your S.O.S. Conversation with a clear focus on the issue:

Performance Problem: Consistent tardiness. "Sean, my expectation is that everyone on the team is here at 8:00 a.m. to start work. I'm concerned because you consistently choose to show up fifteen to thirty minutes late nearly every day. Talk to me about that."

Performance Problem: Teammate in-fighting or conflict. "Ramona and Gigi, as you know, I expect everyone on the team to hold and maintain professional working relationships with each other. You two are showing signs that this is a struggle for you both, and it's negatively impacting the rest of the team. Gigi, let's start with you. How do you see it?"

Performance Problem: Missed deadlines. "Sam, in looking at your work on the water project, I've been clear that deadlines are critical, and I'm expecting everyone to meet each one. I'm concerned because you've missed three of the last five. Talk to me about that."

You'll notice I have a pattern. That's totally fine. Our brains love patterns. When you can work your own pattern, you'll find the practice becomes easier, and you'll be able to frame your issues quicker, diminishing your prep time and getting through the S.O.S. Conversations faster and with less hesitation.

Tips for Identifying Your Issue

In Step 1, Identify Your Issue, remember these key points:

- **Be specific: Get clear and concise about what your issue is.** Think about the words you're going to choose to open the conversation and the effects they are likely to have.

- **Less is more: Don't overtalk it.** When we're in the moment, and we're feeling anxious or tense about the conversation, some of us tend to take a long time getting to the point. We couch our thoughts and sugarcoat the information. Out of respect for the individual and the relationship, get to the point. The more you talk, the more threads and details you invite into the conversation, which can result in a conversation about things you did not intend as well as losing focus on the matter of ownership.

- **Don't judge: Be explicit and curious.** Do not assume you know what's going on, and don't judge the situation preemptively, even if you think you know what's going on. This is how miscommunications and bad feelings get brought into the mix. Create the space for a dialogue.

CHAPTER 7

Step 2: Analyze the Choice Point

ACCOUNTABILITY S.O.S.™ STEP 2

Figure 15

AFTER YOU'RE CLEAR on what your issue is, begin to think about why the other person is delivering or performing as they are. We all have recognizable patterns to how each of us executes our work every day; those patterns offer a useful framework for analyzing a person's performance.

An essential skill in accountability is to accurately identify the point at which a person fails expectations, because that choice point determines the kind of accountability conversation you're going to have. Correctly identifying the choice point provides the platform for how you engage the conversation so as to make it more productive and more readily yield ownership about the exact right thing. The framework I use to determine the correct choice point is called the Performance Drivers & Choice Points model (see figure 16). It illuminates the pattern in the way we perform and encourages us to think critically in order to identify the choice point.

Performance Drivers and Choice Points

Why do people deliver the kind of results they deliver? If you're going to get good at accountability, it will help to have a framework from which to understand and analyze the individual components that go into delivering a performance (i.e., the *how* that leads to the *what*). To be highly successful managing both your own performance and the performance of others, it is essential that you accurately anticipate where that performance is going wrong.

The best way to analyze performance problems is to work from the end result back through all the performance drivers to source the *point of default*. You're essentially attempting to determine at what point the person likely made a choice that didn't work. Remember, this isn't about making assumptions. You're simply evaluating what led to the performance or result. By carefully examining these choice points, you can begin to understand an individual's behaviors, skills, attitudes, beliefs, and values and determine where a poor choice may have occurred. Then, you'll be able to analyze performance and determine the best approach to ownership, accountability, and change. In other words, when you work this model, you'll not only anticipate the most appropriate approach to the S.O.S. Conversation, but you'll also anticipate what changes need to occur to improve a person's performance and results. The aim is to assist a person in lifting their performance in a workable, constructive way.

PERFORMANCE DRIVERS & CHOICE POINTS™

AT WHAT POINT IS THE PERSON MAKING A POOR CHOICE?

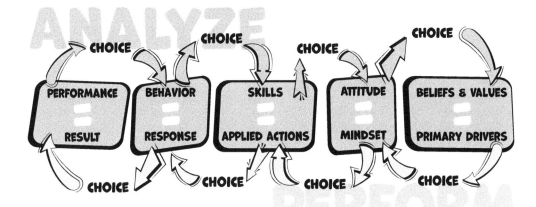

Figure 16

Let's work through the model from left to right, defining our terms as we go.

A Performance Is a Result

Exactly what is a performance? It is the *how* that leads to the result. For example, when you go to the theater, the spectacle you see is the result of all the prior rehearsing of the actors, the casting, the lighting, the costumes, the choreography or staging—everything that enables the fully coordinated show on the night you attend. There have been a series of choices made by all involved to deliver the final performance. It's the same at work. For example, when a customer is satisfied with how they are treated, it's the result of a team member delivering their best performance in customer service. They've made the best choices of skills and behaviors in managing that customer. The performance and ultimately the result are driven by a series of *choices*, and those choices are driven by behaviors.

A Behavior Is a Response

A behavior is a thought-out, or thought-full, response to any given situation. It's different from a reaction insofar as reactions are actions taken without any real thought. For example, a customer calls and is irate regarding the lack of service or attention to their account; depending on how many robots they had to talk to and buttons they had to push prior to reaching a human person, their state of aggravation is most likely very high. The customer service representative must offer an immediate response. Choosing how to respond is critical to how the customer receives the response. Therefore, the representative must *choose* the best response from a series of options. The way that representative chooses to respond is a reflection of their skills. In other words, they draw from their customer service skills to select an appropriate response.

> The performance and ultimately the result are driven by a series of *choices*, and those choices are driven by behaviors.

A Skill Is an Application

Skills are applied in the actions we take; they are something we do or act out. A series or combination of skills is usually required to enact a behavior, and it takes a series or combination of behaviors to generate a performance that achieves the desired result.

We all have different sets of skills, or what we call a "skill bank." An individual's skill bank is created by that individual's interests, knowledge, experience, and internal drive. It is made by *choice*. Just because we attended the training, that doesn't mean we're going to adopt the skill or practice. Just because management would like all the tellers to gin up interest in other banking services doesn't mean that every teller will actually do it, especially if they do not find value in the task. Behind that choice, the primary component of determining what forms a skill bank is attitude.

An Attitude Is a Mindset

A person's attitude or mindset speaks to their experience, and how they feel about that experience. Our attitude or mindset affects the choices we make to develop our own individual skills bank. For example, it is unlikely that an individual will be highly skilled as a customer service provider if that person has a negative attitude about the value of dealing with people. Our bank teller, hired for a transactional position, may not succeed when asked to perform sales-related behaviors like inquiring about customers' mortgage needs and the like. A teller who has no interest in upselling or cross-selling people who've simply come in to make deposits or withdrawals will not invest in skills to engage people in a sales conversation. Flight attendants whose primary interests are safety and service may not succeed at selling credit card applications during a flight. Our attitudes are a choice. We generally choose to develop skills around the things we care about, the things we feel have value. Those choices are driven by one's beliefs and values, what one holds to be true and important.

Primary Performance Drivers Are Beliefs and Values

The engine that generates your performance choices begins with your beliefs and values. It's important to consider both. When I train managers using this model, I ask the questions: "What is a belief?" and "What is a value?" The variety of answers I get indicates that these aren't terms we often have to think about defining. Some of us are not clear on the difference. But it's important to know and recognize that there is a difference, and both beliefs and values are in play all the time in our decision-making.

Simply stated, our values are what we hold to be important. Company values, for example, are declarations made by your organization to tell you what it sees as important. These, of course, play into building the culture the company wants. They are indicators and guides telling us what's okay and what's not okay regarding how we show up. Beliefs are something else entirely; they're what we hold to be true. Not everyone shares the same truth, as we've become well aware from our use of social media. In accountability conversations, sometimes poor decisions come from holding on to, or operating from, a *truth* that may not be true, or a *truth* that may not be shared. Do not worry about that. *An S.O.S. Conversation never requires you to try to change someone's truth.* It does, however, demand that you identify when a person is operating against organizational values or if there is a conflict around beliefs that is negatively impacting performance. People are most often hired for their demonstrated experience—their skills and behaviors—and more often fired for ongoing conflicts and sustained performance problems related to mindsets, values, and beliefs.

Focus On Choices

When analyzing a person's performance, you work from the result back to behaviors, back to skills, back to attitudes, then back to beliefs and values to determine answers to questions like: Did the individual have the appropriate skills but choose the wrong behavior? Did they choose the only behavior they could, given their limited skill bank? Did they know the appropriate behavior? Did they know the skills required but make a poor choice due to an inappropriate attitude about managing the result?

It's easy to think that people's beliefs and values are at the heart of why they show up and deliver the way that they do, but I want to emphasize that the most important part of this backward-stepping process is the focus on *choices* (see figure 16). That is where all the answers are—and where all the power sits—in the choices we make. The whole point of this framework is to identify the choice point for a poor performance result.

Let's return to one of the examples we looked at earlier—where the performance result was *sloppy work*. Following the model, let's look at behavior first. Has this person delivered excellent, neat, and error-free work previously on a similar project? If their work always has some level of inattention, then perhaps they've got a self-destructive behavior (procrastination or last-minuting) or a lack of skills around proofreading, fact-checking, grammar, spelling, or whatever the project entails. This would indicate that you should approach your conversation from choice points centered around behaviors and skills, in that this is where you anticipate they have made a faulty choice.

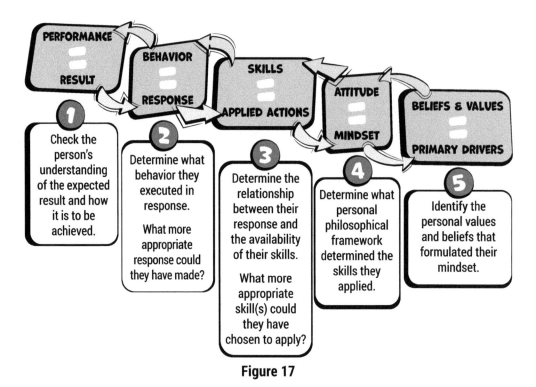

Figure 17

That conversation starts like this:

I wanted to talk to you about the quality of your work. My expectation is that you submit neatly formatted documents that are proofread both for spelling and grammar as well as fact-checked with your team to ensure accurate and timely information. I'm concerned because you consistently submit work that has errors in one or more of these areas. Can you talk to me about that?

If you have seen better and acceptable work from this person previously on similar projects, then you already know they have the behaviors and skills to deliver the expected results. In this case, you might anticipate that they are choosing not to use those, which is to say that their choice is driven by their attitude (how they've judged their task or the project as a whole, or by how you've engaged or disengaged them) or beliefs and values (what they actually see as more important—a different project or task—or what they see as true about the work, the team, or you). This can happen when someone becomes disengaged or has conflicting priorities. Perhaps they were not appointed team lead on a project and feel strongly that they were the best candidate for the role. Perhaps they are on multiple projects and serve many masters.

If they are feeling unrecognized or overlooked and underappreciated, they're making choices from an emotional place rather than a rational one—letting apathy or anger drive their decision-making. In that case, too, the choice point is centered around attitude or beliefs and values. Perhaps they've got an attitude that says, "Well, if I'm not seen as important, then this project is no longer important to me, so who cares what it looks like. Let the team lead fix it, since they're so fantastic." Or perhaps they are not conflicted about how they are perceived within the organization and may be acting out of anger or spite by not giving their full effort.

That conversation starts like this:

I wanted to talk to you about the quality of your work. My expectation is that you submit neatly formatted documents that are proofread both for spelling and grammar as well as fact-checked with your team to ensure accurate and timely information. I'm concerned because you've done such excellent work previously. I get the sense that you're upset about the role you've been assigned on this project. Can you talk to me about that?

An example of a values issue is a person who is always late to a specific meeting. They know what time the meeting starts. They know it's important to be on time, and they value how they are perceived. Yet they consistently choose to be late because they've deemed their time to be of greater value than the meeting. Choice points around beliefs and values are indicative of conflict around what is true and what is important.

A value conflict can lead to performance choices where a team member may overtalk other team members, take over in a meeting, and attempt to make decisions for the team. This may be because this person actually believes they are *the* expert and so acts as such, to the detriment of the team.

In your opening to the accountability conversation, you both identify the issue and analyze the choice point where you think the detrimental choice is happening. You might get it wrong from time to time, but that's perfectly okay because you're having a conversation about clarity. If you've gotten it wrong, you'll be corrected by the other person.

> In your opening to the accountability conversation, you both identify the issue and analyze the choice point where you think the detrimental choice is happening.

For example, if you were to use that last conversation opener we reviewed, and the person responds with a look of surprise and says, *"No. I'm not unhappy at all with my role on the project. I'm just slammed with competing priorities and don't have the time,"* then you'll know you're working from another choice point. The whole exercise of anticipating the choice point is to engage the question: What would have been a better choice? That is where solution-based thinking and action begins.

Choice Point Location Determines Time and Effort

The choice point helps you determine the most effective approach to the conversation. Choice points to the left of attitude are a training or coaching approach, while choice points taken at attitude or beliefs and values (to the right) require a counseling approach (see figure 18.) The further back you go within the framework, meaning the further away (to the right on the model) the choice point is from the performance/result, the more difficult it becomes for you to change that performance result, and the more time and work it requires. When you are dealing with a choice point around beliefs and values, you are essentially dealing with conflict about what's important and true for the individual, for you, and/ or for the organization. That's where your harder management decisions are located, in terms of how much time and effort you can afford to put into someone who may be in a sustained conflict, meaning they may never hold to be important what you or the company hold to be important. For example, they are not a fit if they are unwilling to own the conflict they've got, deal with that conflict, resolve it, and move forward. The company, the division, the team, or you are most likely not going to change to meet their needs in this regard. If they are willing to own the conflict and make an effort to resolve it, as long as this is happening within a time frame that you consider reasonable, know that it is possible for a person to turn a corner and get back on board relatively quickly. And sometimes, it just takes a person realizing they've got the conflict in the first place to know how to handle it appropriately. Some conflict arises when a person's willingness stays at bay because they'd really prefer or are comfortable with doing something else. A lot of people prefer comfort and familiarity over change and therefore become unwilling or conflicted about the *new* ask or improvement presented to them.

PERFORMANCE DRIVERS & CHOICE POINTS™

AT WHAT POINT IS THE PERSON MAKING A POOR CHOICE?

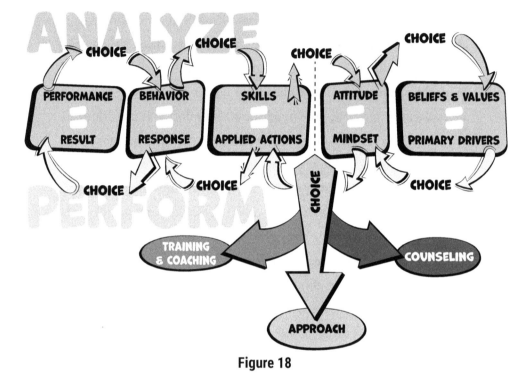

Figure 18

Let's expand on that earlier conversation. This time, I want to track what's happening within the dialogue.

Manager	*I wanted to talk to you about the quality of your work. My expectation is that you submit neatly formatted documents that are proofread both for spelling and grammar as well as fact-checked with your team to ensure accurate and timely information. I'm concerned because you've done such excellent work previously. I get the sense that you're upset about the role you've been assigned on this project. Can you talk to me about that?*	Anticipated choice point = Attitude
Employee	*No. I'm not unhappy at all with my role on the project. I'm just slammed with competing priorities and just don't have the time.*	Answer reflects a behavioral choice
Manager	*I understand. When you knew your quality was slipping, what did you choose to do?*	Probing for actual choice
Employee	*What do you mean? I don't know. I probably just called it done and moved on.*	Not clear on choice
Manager	*Go back in your mind. Think about it for a minute. You're reviewing the document and maybe you're thinking this will just have to do, or something along those lines. What did you do?*	Probing again, to ascertain actual thinking
Employee	*Well, I was probably tired. I remember doing this work at the end of the day. And I probably thought, of all the things I'm trying to get done, this project doesn't have the same level of visibility as the other work, so I just figured it wouldn't be that important. Then I just let it go out that way.*	Clarity and ownership of the choice made and the reason why

Manager	*I see. I understand. In thinking about it now, what might have been a better choice?*	Probing for clarity and ownership of the expectation—better behavioral choice(s)
Employee	*Well, I probably shouldn't assume that project visibility or importance determines the level of accuracy. The standard applies to all my work.*	Clear ownership
Manager	*Right. We all have high levels of work, and it can sometimes feel crushing. What do you think would help you when this comes up again?*	Move the conversation to practical problem-solving and mutual understanding about better options.

Five Scenarios

Here are a few scenarios for you to test your ability to analyze and anticipate the choice point for beginning the S.O.S. Conversation.

Scenario One:

You have a direct report on your team who continually reprioritizes the workload/tasks she's responsible for completing. She chooses to do the work she enjoys most, leaving other tasks out. This inevitably leaves her teammates to pick up the slack. Teammates are complaining about this person.

Choice Point:

Most likely between attitude and skills. Why? Because she's got demonstrated ability to do the work but is choosing not to. She may feel that because the teammates have been able to pick up the slack, they'll continue to do so. She may even have the perspective that they enjoy doing those tasks. Additionally, you've got a skills issue with your team regarding their inability to hold her accountable to begin with.

Scenario Two:

You have a team lead who creates a bottleneck getting work product finished and sent over to another team. The work is consistently good and error-free, which is important for the kind of work your team does. Your team leader wants to move up in the organization, but you cannot see how he'll be able to handle the increased scope of work.

Choice Point:

Most likely between behavior and performance. Why? This high level of integrity around work product is evidence of his ambition. It may also be a destructive behavior; perhaps it's perfectionism. While it's not oppressive toward those on his team, it may be obsessive for him and may potentially cost him a promotion.

Scenario Three:

You've got a long-term manager who has been great at leading her previous team. She's six months into managing a new team of high performers, and things are going sideways in ways you did not anticipate. There is more in-fighting and conflict among team members, and team results are starting to be delayed, which is also impacting customers.

Choice Point:

Most likely between skills and behaviors. Why? Because conflict is indicative of a lack of clarity. She may lack the skills to deal with work conflict, so she lets it ride too long or doesn't address it directly. She may also lack skills for setting clear expectations or delegating appropriately.

Scenario Four:

You've got a highly experienced manager who knows his part of the business inside and out. He's been in his role a long time, and he's looked to move to a different role over the past two years. He has applied for higher-level open positions in the company that would promote him and challenge his capabilities; however, he has yet to be selected for promotion. He's been training up new hires and continuing to complete the work required of him and his team. During the last full-court press on tight deadlines, you noticed that he only worked his regular forty hours but did not put in any extra time or effort to meet deadlines or support his team to accomplish tasks. He left it with them. You've also noticed that he engages less with his peers. There's been a lot of turnover in your area. You don't want to lose him too.

Choice Point:

Most likely between beliefs and values and attitude. Why? He may be harboring some resentment that he cannot get promoted. So he may have decided to work the baseline requirements of the job and disengage from all discretionary effort. He may no longer see the point.

Scenario Five:

You've got a peer who leads another team that interacts directly with your team to provide final product for your customer. When you are in meetings with the boss, your peer often throws you under the bus when discussing customer issues or product delays, indicating your team is at fault. You both know that neither team is performing well, based on recent project discussions.

Choice Point:

Could be between behavior and performance or between attitude and skill. Why? If it's behavioral, the choice may be about controlling the narrative for himself and his team. If it's attitude, then the choice may be about results over relationships; perhaps he doesn't care about hurting the relationship when it comes down to it.

Tips for Analyzing the Choice Point

In Step 2, Analyze the Choice Point, remember these key points:

- **Always work backward from results to primary drivers**. Don't assume you know exactly what's going on. When you think it through honestly and critically, you may surprise yourself with your ability to more effectively uncover what might actually be going on for the other person.

- **The purpose of the choice point is to indicate the appropriate approach to the conversation**. Targeted conversations are more productive in achieving ownership and accountability because there's less wiggle room for blaming, minimizing, or sidestepping poor results or bad behaviors and less room for talking in circles and getting nowhere.

- **Regardless of where the choice point occurs, you can effectively gain ownership**. Utilizing the framework increases your skill and, more important, your confidence about how you engage the conversation. Knowing that you can achieve ownership at any choice point allows you to support people by giving them the opportunity to change how they're showing up to your team or company.

- **Invite critical thinking about choices, not agreement or compliance**. The whole point of accountability is clarity and ownership. It's about driving down the right road, not about the imagined destination. In other words, you don't start an accountability conversation with the thought of the outcome, *I need Joe to own his bad team behavior and apologize to the team.* For Joe to take ownership, he has to arrive for himself at the point of clarity. Joe needs to examine his team behavior and think about how he can improve it quickly. The better you are at getting the person to think critically about the issues you've presented, the better the clarity and ownership become not only about the performance itself, but also about any solutions they may be able to provide. For you, the critical thinking comes both before you open your mouth in an accountability conversation as well as during it. For the other person, the critical thinking is summoned by how you set the table. It's the dish they are encouraged to bring.

CHAPTER 8

Step 3: Explore the Impacts

Figure 19

AN IMPORTANT STEP you take on your way to engaging in an accountability conversation is taking time to think through the impacts of the poor choice, poor performance, and unmet expectation.

To begin, it's the impacts that make the issue real and significant. If there are no impacts to not meeting an expectation, how important can it be? It's insulting to be held accountable for unmet expectations that have no meaningful bearing on relationships or work products. If your expectation is "just do this because I want you to do it," that's nothing but an issue of power and control for you. Clarifying impacts creates a stronger context for the importance of the expectation and why it's there to begin with. That should allow the other person to see the bigger picture of how their choices play into their relationship with you and the larger expectations and results of the team, division, or organization as a whole.

Impacts Create Urgency

Introducing impacts helps to illustrate the severity of poor performance choices—the magnitude of performance issues. They're what make the issue to be addressed more or less compelling in terms of the need to create a solution.

It's helpful to think about impacts from a peer-to-peer standpoint in which you've got unmet expectations from a teammate or another division. What may be huge and compelling for you might be minor and less consequential for your peer. How you frame the impacts your peer is generating with their choices will help it matter not just to you but to them as well. If you come to your peer illustrating only the impacts within your own organization, limited to your own self-interest, how much ownership will your peer really take? They'll have a reasonable excuse for why they did not do what you expected them to do or why their team did not deliver to your team as expected, and furthermore, they'll expect you to deal with and manage things on your own team.

When considering impacts in a case like this one, look at the larger framework. What is important to your peer? Can you connect impacts to things that matter to them in addition to what matters to you? Can you determine what's personally important to them, to who they are or how they see themselves? For example: Say the issue is that you cannot get timely information from your peer in order to generate a report that goes up to the top team for next quarter decision-making. Your peer's name is not on the report. It is one of many areas of the business that drives data. You're always having to work last-minute on the final report because your peer regularly misses deadlines for data. How do you create urgency for them?

Here's how you might create urgency by making it personal:

Hi, Vicky, thanks for taking time to meet with me. I want to raise an issue I've got with how we're working together on generating the quarterly report. My expectation is that all the key data areas deliver their numbers to me five days out from the quarterly meeting. I'm concerned because you are consistent in delivering yours late. The impact this is having is not only on my team, where we're having to do the eleventh-hour hustle to include your data, but it's also diminishing your credibility with the others who submit information—in particular, those whose names go on this report. The concern is around accuracy. While we double-check what we can, we don't have the time needed to feel confident. Can you talk to me about that?

By including what may be at stake for the other person over the long term, without shaming or blaming, you'll introduce an impact they may not be considering when they're making decisions about their own work priorities. It's also important to remember this is said without judgment and with an intention to offer support and build solutions.

Impacts Build Leverage

Impacts must be real and visible. Clarity about impacts should make what's invisible visible; in so doing, it should create leverage for taking ownership. In other words, impacts should matter to the person from whom you are seeking accountability. Sometimes there are obvious impacts. You can use the obvious, but look deeper too. Generally, it's the deeper impacts that are more compelling. The most powerful leverage is created when you can connect the dots of impact regarding things that are not only important to you, the team, and the company but to the person individually, regarding something they value directly.

I cannot emphasize this enough: building leverage with impacts is not about shaming. Don't go looking for pain points to shame someone into accountability. *You are not effective if you exploit someone's emotional exposure by leveraging their vulnerability.* When you do that, you are just an asshole. Instead, be a trusted advisor. Your duty is to push up against their values in a way that causes them to examine the impact, and you should approach that responsibility from a place of support, not power. The question is not: "How can I make you feel badly about this and yourself?" The question is: "*How can I help you protect yourself, show up stronger, and continue to add value by increasing your capability?*"

For example, and returning again to the *sloppy work* issue, a potentially potent impact you might leverage would be the creation of rework for other team members, thereby connecting the impact to their team relationships. You could also leverage the potential or real impacts of diminished trustworthiness or credibility as a team member, thereby connecting the impact to their sense of self-worth. These are as important as the more obvious impacts of this person having to go back on their own to spend time reviewing as well as missing a deadline. When you explore impacts from a people-positive perspective, you activate the other person's intention to do a good job. Most people come to work to do a good job.

Here's an example of what that would sound like:

"I wanted to talk to you about the quality of your work. As you know, my expectation is that you submit neatly formatted documents that are proofread both for spelling and grammar as well as fact-checked with your team to ensure accurate and timely information. I'm concerned because you've done such excellent work previously. I'm also concerned because the impact of this has been primarily on your teammates who are having to do rework on your part of the project. It not only impacts the team's work; I see that it's also impacting their ability to trust your work. Can you talk to me about that?"

Ownership for performance goes beyond tasks to include behaviors and work relationships. Awareness of the impacts on all fronts is critical for improved results and growth—both for the individual and for the business.

Tips for Exploring the Impacts

In Step 3, Explore the Impacts, remember these key points:

- **Impacts provide better context**. Context around performance is what makes it meaningful for people to get on board. When we know more about how we are seen and experienced, we have more at stake. As I mentioned earlier, it's more important than pretty much anything else for us to feel connected. Context around performance lets us see how well we are connecting. Most of us want to do better.

- **Impacts create urgency**. Who doesn't have the need for speed when it comes to getting work done? Identifying performance impacts builds a little fire under people to put in the effort not only to take ownership for the results but to take ownership for improvement. It's what we, in the coaching business, call "keeping the discontent hot." The impetus for people to change is never really about the rainbow at the end or about how much better things will be overall. Change is more often driven by the discontent we feel about where we are. For example, if I'm twenty pounds overweight, it's not the new clothes I will get when I am skinnier that will motivate me, or how good I will feel when I'm healthier. Instead, what gets me going is how crappy I feel now. What motivates me to change is not wanting to fight to bend down to put on my shoes or cram my butt into an airplane seat.

CHAPTER 9

Step 4: Prepare and Rehearse

Figure 20

WE ALL KNOW what it means to rehearse—it's an informal rundown, a trying out, running through, or going over. How you speak to people in the moment—especially in the moments that matter—is what separates the professionals from the amateurs. And what separates the professionals from amateurs is preparation and practice! We tell ourselves that we are for the most part effective, but that's likely because nobody has given us feedback about how we're not clear or consistent in our accountability conversations.

Accountability conversations have a certain luster of specialness; because they are so infrequent, the fact that they're stilted or uncomfortable or rambling ends up being tolerated. But the truth of the matter is that if you are good at accountability conversations, you step into them with ease and confidence that's earned through preparation. And the only way to get to that point is to practice first—not just in your head, but on paper and out loud. Especially when you're first trying out this new way of talking, write your script. Practice it out loud. Practice it with your coach. Practice it until you feel you have a good handle on how to invite the conversation with ease.

Will it happen in real time the way you scripted it? Of course not. But if you've followed the six steps of the S.O.S. Conversation, what you say should be close enough to what you scripted for you to stay focused and on point. I'm going to lay out the benefits of Step 4 because I know from my coaching practice that this is the step you'll hate and want to skip. Intellectually, you've got accountability down, and that's because it's easy enough to understand. But understanding is only half the job. You can read the book or watch the YouTube video on how to do something. However, and as you know, when you're actually doing that thing, it's a whole other thing. *As an adult learner, you will only achieve better skills at applying yourself in real time if you make time and take time to practice.*

When I'm teaching in a group setting, I regularly see this transformation happen. I review the concepts, and everyone is pleased. Then I ask for a demonstration: "Who wants to start the conversation?" The room gets quiet. Eye contact is averted—it's no different from a middle school classroom. I select a participant who begrudgingly steps up to the plate, all eyes on them. Then, they dive in. Ninety-nine percent of the time, what happens is either a somewhat tentative stab at identifying an issue or an all-inclusive rambling missive, depending on the personality. But then comes the improvisational work of problem-solving out loud and in action. The idea that I hope takes hold in that moment is that the S.O.S. Conversation is not an exercise in winging it but an attempt to work within conversational guardrails in order to apply a model and a set of skills to a given situation.

As they hear themselves speak and finish setting the table around the issue, they are the first to acknowledge: "Oh, that didn't sound quite right," or "Oh, wait a minute, let me do that again. I was all over the place." They can hear it. On the off chance that they *can't* hear it, others in the room can, which is why it's great to practice with a trusted coworker or coach. We are so eloquent in our heads! We can visualize ourselves engaging successfully. While visualization is a good ability, it's not enough in this instance. For many of us, it's going to take

> The S.O.S. Conversation is not an exercise in winging it but an attempt to work within conversational guardrails in order to apply a model and a set of skills to a given situation.

checking in with someone who understands Steps 1 through 3 so as not to miss the mark on gaining ownership for the choice we actually need the person to take accountability for. The primary benefit of Step

4 is hearing yourself out loud so that you can identify flaws in both your word choice and your thinking.

After all, there are essentially three things you can get wrong in an accountability conversation: your thinking, your word choice, and your nonverbals and paralinguistics. Does your physical self say the same thing as what you are expressing verbally? Do your breathing, articulation, tempo, pronunciation, intonation, and speed work to support your message, or do these add emphasis and shades of meaning that betray your best intentions?

The secondary benefit of Step 4 is that it's a confidence builder. As you work to feel more comfortable and on point with the way you begin the dialogue, the process of the practice forces you to try out several versions to see which one seems best. With each attempt, you'll create more clarity about the issue and your expectations. You'll develop the muscle memory that will ultimately allow for more agility during the actual conversation. The more you know and understand what you are asking and looking for, the more options you'll start to see for framing the conversation so that it works.

Rehearsal is different from performing before a live audience. When you get eyeball to eyeball across from the person you are going to hold accountable, the energy in the room is impacted by how they perceive you, and that impacts how you sense the moment. What felt safe in rehearsal can feel unsafe in actual practice. To regain the feeling of safety, your words help to change—or in this case, control—your state of mind. As you begin the conversation that you practiced, those words allow your brain to move out of that lizard-driven amygdala if you need to, or they allow you to remain in the prefrontal cortex, keeping you focused and able to listen. When you're no longer rehearsing, listening to how the person responds is as important as how you begin the conversation; it's what will indicate where you go next. If you're feeling unsafe, you may not really hear the other person, you may assume you hear, or worse, you may hear what you want to hear in order to stay safe.

You've likely started to see that all of these steps work in concert. For example, if you just do Step 4, you'll be practicing a whole encounter that may not actually be about the issue you think it is. So don't skip the first three steps.

Up Your Game with a DiSC Assessment

Think of the DiSC as your road map for accountability language and rehearsal. It's the stage for your performance. You want to make an entrance and hold the space effectively. A communication style assessment is your best bet for success.

Earlier, I noted that you'll have an advantage in communicating with others if you're both familiar with your own communication style and have a firm grasp on the communication styles of others. Has your organization already invested in a similar tool? If so, learn it. Ideally, everyone on your team would have taken the assessment, so you know what everyone's default style is. It's not just a treasure trove for how to approach people and build relationships; it also offers inside information on how best to communicate when the pressure is on. I work with Everything DiSC, which is a portfolio of assessments that dive into more than just basic communication styles to provide assessments around managing (delegating, motivating, etc.), leading (challenges and strengths for vision, alignment, and execution), emotional agility, productive conflict, and teams.

And even if you're the only one in your business who's taken a DiSC assessment, you'll be more self-aware about how you show up for others, including how you are most likely experienced and perceived, and more aware of how others may be different from you.

As a leader and manager, it is your degree of flexibility to lean into the other styles that can make you effective with others. Learn the whole DiSC, not just what is important to your communication style.

Figure 21

For example, if I am a D style, which is dominant, I'm going to be very results oriented and like it when everyone is brief and can cut to the chase. These inclinations of mine can feel impersonal and blunt to the S style, steadiness, who is more collaborative and harmony seeking. So if I've got to give an S-style employee some tough feedback about underperforming, I will surely create a problem if I speak to them in my preferred style. My perspective might be: "Why can't they just do their job? Why do I have to pussyfoot around with all this *caring and sharing* when they should be up to the task of getting feedback from me. It's part of the job!" If I'm someone who's motivated by power, authority, competition, winning, and success, it's helpful for me to understand that flexing to more of an S style of communication in that moment increases my chance of success as well as gives me additional impact power as a leader or manager.

Accountability conversations for an S style, who is motivated by stable environments, sincere appreciation, cooperation, and opportunities to help, can be difficult because S tends to couch difficult information; their worries about creating discord can make it be uncomfortable for them to be clear. The challenge increases when they are managing a D style, who just wants you to give it to them straight. So an S will need to practice out loud giving feedback straight and clear without all the cushioning and supportive interjections. For them, it's important to understand how that will be a better form of support for a D.

I mention these two styles because they tend to struggle most when it comes to talking with others about accountability, but the DiSC assessment can help you prepare and rehearse no matter where you or your conversation partner fall within the four primary categories.

Tips for Preparing and Rehearsing

In Step 4, Prepare and Rehearse, remember these key points:

- **Speaking off the cuff does not guarantee clarity; most of the time it impedes it.** Make sure you're taking the time to think critically about what the issue is and putting that forth clearly as a way to open the conversation. Speaking off the cuff is generally reactive or based on an assumption about what you feel or sense is going on; it's too reliant on instinct and your own past experience. When you submit to your assumptions or your own impatience or intolerance, you forgo critical thinking and preliminary analysis. Instead, step outside yourself to examine the unmet expectation—the *why* of the situation and not just the *what*. If you feel that you are highly articulate or have the "gift of the gab" and can talk your way through any situation, know that that feeling can be a hinderance. When it comes to the S.O.S. Conversation, you'll most likely overtalk your issue and create confusion as you ramble on out of your own discomfort—a discomfort that may even have appeared unexpectedly regardless of your speaking prowess and your familiarity or history with the person who you now find yourself having to hold accountable.

- **Rehearsing develops a better script; it ensures that you have the right words when you need them.** Accountability is a communication skill. Having a clear sense of the language you need for the conversation is the best preparation. *Having words that accurately address the situation allows those words to serve as handholds when you feel emotionally vulnerable.* They act as a ballast when you sense emotional intensity or when the conversation may be going off course or in a negative direction. Knowing the language by heart provides you with guardrails for keeping the conversation focused and on track. Knowing the language you want to use allows you to speak with intention and with a stronger sense of how what you say will sound or be interpreted by the other person.

- **Rehearsing forces you to imagine how the other person will respond, which allows you to be more strategic and less reactive.** Part of the emotional response to accountability conversations is the fear of the unknown. When you practice the conversation, you gain confidence by thinking through how the other person will most likely respond. It's rare when we can't imagine how things will go. Most of the time, we are speaking with people we know, with whom we've worked, and have some sense in terms of their style or personality to give us insight into how they're most likely to react.

- **Rehearsing allows us to tap our insight and work out multiple ways to engage while staying focused on accountability and ownership.** Rehearsing gives you the conversational muscle you need to anticipate outcomes as opposed to merely reacting. It also allows you the comfort and the time to think about what to say, should you be thrown a curve ball you don't expect.

- **Rehearsing increases your ability to stay focused in the moment.** Conversational agility is a sign of communication mastery. Keeping focused isn't about being rigid or ignoring what's said that may take the conversation in another direction. It's about acknowledging what's been said but then pivoting back to the point in a way that shows you're paying attention, that's respectful, and that keeps the conversation engaging. If you're shutting the other person down or instigating an amygdala hijack, you're not doing it correctly.

- **Rehearsing improves your ability to anticipate responses and primes you to listen.** It's listening that validates whether the other person is responding the way you anticipated or differently. On stage, actors know whose turn it is to speak. But occasionally, an actor "goes up," meaning they forget their line or, worse, they drop a line that's a cue for another character. The other actors must always be listening attentively: Did I hear my cue? If I didn't, because I'm listening, I know exactly where we are in the action and can continue the dialogue. Rehearsal in preparation for your S.O.S. Conversation allows you to do the same sort of attentive listening to exactly what you're hearing and then move the conversation along in the direction you intend it to go. Are you hearing ownership? Is it denial? Is it ownership with a "but" clause that really indicates no ownership, as in: "Yes, I see what you mean, and of course, *but* Bryant didn't really have his work done to spec, so I couldn't finish."

CHAPTER 10

Step 5: Engage the Conversation

Figure 22

WELCOME TO STEP FIVE, where you're ready to have the conversation. By now, you should be feeling well prepared. You're ready to engage the other person in dialogue and to listen and respond in real time. We've spent the first four steps focused on you to get you ready to include someone else's thoughts and perspectives. Accountability, as you now know for certain, is not a one-way experience; it's not just about you and how you see things, how you want or need things to be. Let's review together the most important aspects of the dialogue.

Be Timely

Accountability conversations are not conversations that you save for later. Just because there are four steps ahead of this one doesn't mean you take a week to think all that through and practice. It might take you forty-five minutes or an hour when you're getting started, but you should eventually be able to think things through and engage in practice in fifteen minutes. In other words, don't use Steps 1 through 4 as a reason to take forever to get to Step 5. You are smart enough to figure it all out and run through it. Your timeliness matters because the longer you allow the confusion or lack of accountability to linger within your team, your department, your division, or your project, the more you increase the odds that it will be more difficult to deal with. Things change over time. What begins as a problem will, over time, escalate into conflict.

On that note, let's take just a minute to distinguish problems from conflicts. Problems are rational by nature; you think them through, and you devise solutions to deal with them. Then, you apply those solutions, evaluate the results, and then make changes to ensure the best outcome is achieved. Conflicts are emotionally driven and involve unresolved feelings. You cannot problem solve conflicts. Conflicts are *resolved* by being *let go of*. When you let go of a conflict, it essentially means you don't feel a heightened negative emotion anymore.

As managers, we are habitually drawn to problem-solving because it's what we are paid to do. It's what our direct reports come to us for most of the time, so it tends to characterize how we see the world. We show up every day and solve problems for the team and the business.

However, if we've not been the best at holding others accountable—doing it well and consistently—the situation will morph over time. Take, for example, a member of the team who consistently shows up late or is never prepared for meetings. In the beginning, these things are problematic for you or the other team members, but over time, if accountability conversations have not taken place, the chances that this behavior will escalate into a conflict is high. A problem escalates from a rationally addressable issue (meaning something that could easily be solved by discussion and by agreeing to a solution once the individual takes ownership) into a conflict (meaning that it's now an emotionally driven issue because teammates are angry about the ongoing behavior, its impacts, and its implications).

> You cannot problem solve conflicts.

Think of this in terms of the Performance Drivers & Choice Points model that we discussed earlier (see figure 23). It's like the issue has moved from the left to the right, shifting further away from performance toward attitude and thereby crossing the line from a coaching scenario into counseling. People can remain in conflict for a very long period of time. It's harder work to resolve conflict, which means you've got to be patient with people while they work through letting go. If you've been the manager who allowed something to go on for too long and other direct reports are now angry about that, the *letting go* process will necessitate the rebuilding of trust with your team. That's the trust you broke when, out of trepidation, anxiety, lack of focus, or for whatever reason, you did not put the needs of the team as a whole before your own need to avoid feeling emotionally vulnerable. Put another way, you can break trust with your team when you don't stand in the moment of holding a person accountable in a timely manner when they are impacting the team in a negative way. Over time, avoiding holding underperformers accountable will also drive away your best talent and top performers.

PERFORMANCE DRIVERS & CHOICE POINTS™

WHEN A PROBLEM SHIFTS TO BECOME A CONFLICT

When your employees have to wait for you to hold someone accountable, you run the risk of creating conflict.

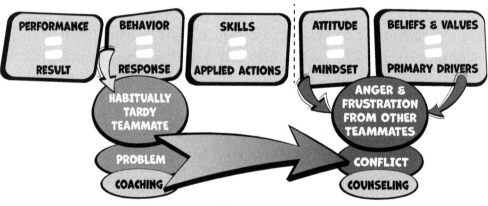

Figure 23

Ownership Is a Response

The most critical part of the accountability conversation is the response. The only reason you have to move through four steps to get here is because you want to narrow the response to two outcomes: acceptance (ownership) of a performance issue or denial of that issue (no ownership). It's that simple. But you have to be able to hear and recognize ownership or the absence thereof.

What does ownership sound like? It sounds like agreement, in full, of everything you've put on the table. Something like "You're absolutely right ... I did that" or "I agree. I need to do better" qualifies as ownership. Keep in mind that the conversation doesn't end at ownership statements. *Full ownership comes with ownership of solutions as well.*

As much as we need to know what acceptance and ownership sound like, we also need to learn to recognize denial because, sadly, more often than not, denial is what we get. We get blaming and excuse-giving for why things went south: "It's not my fault if Liam can't get his stuff to me on time. He's the reason I'm late. You really should be talking to Liam." Or maybe your conversation partner cries or gets defensive and wants to argue with you. These are precisely the responses we dread. They're what keep us from having the accountability conversation in the first place.

Here's the thing: You cannot control this. You can mitigate these responses by getting good at Steps 1 through 3, but you cannot avoid them completely. That's okay because Step 4 has prepared you to anticipate this kind of response and keep your focus. If a person responds defensively, it could very well be their pattern of response, and you would likely know this already and be prepared for it. The important thing to keep in mind is that if they're being defensive, they're expressing denial and rejection of ownership. They are protecting themselves instead of taking up responsibility.

Deal with Denial

Rejection of ownership by way of denial is a critical point in the conversation. This is how accountability conversations get sidetracked onto other things. This is how the conversation you thought you were going to have turns into something completely different from which you may walk away thinking: *How did that happen?* or *Why is it I'm the one doing stuff, and they're not changing anything?* or *Ugh! That was completely pointless!*

In your practice, at Step 4, anticipate denial as the first response. When you are in the conversation, deal with the denial. When I say "deal," I mean hear it and recognize it for what it is. It will sound like blame. It will sound like excuses. It may sound like arguing. It will sound like minimizing or like nothing at all—muteness. An easy way to recognize denial is to know what ownership sounds like. For example, "You are so right. I've stuffed up this project" is ownership. "I know. I'm late every day" is ownership. "Yes, I am consistently late with the documents. I know, and it bothers me"—ownership. *If you don't have clear ownership, what you have is denial.* Sometimes, you can get what we call "partial ownership." That's when, based on the issue you've presented, the response is "yes and no." The other person will be in agreement with some of what you've said and not in agreement with the whole of what you've said. If you get full ownership, you're on to Step 6. If you get partial ownership, you're still on to Step 6. If you get denial, you do what's in the next paragraph.

Dealing with denial is based on your ability to remain focused on the fact that what you heard in response to your issue is not ownership. Confront it. Ask in a nonjudgmental way—with a neutral or curious tone—a clarifying question: "I heard everything you just said. But what I'm really hearing is that you're not willing to take ownership for (or responsibility for) <fill in the blank>. Is that what you're telling me?" When I invite you to "stand in the moment" of accountability, *this is that moment.* It's the moment of clarity when you essentially ask, "Do you take responsibility or not?" But notice how I phrased the question initially. It's a clarifying question, not an aggressive interrogation. It comes from a place of curiosity about the response. It does not come from a place of judgment, anger, frustration, or the desire for power over the other

> **Dealing with denial is based on your ability to remain focused on the fact that what you heard in response to your issue is not ownership. Confront it.**

person. Being curious is safe. The rest of those approaches are not safe. The unsafe path results in arguments, miscommunication, misunderstandings, and then broken trust and broken relationships. *Be warned. Accountability is about clarity, not power and authority.*

"Victim Mentality" Is a Choice

Denial often comes dressed as a victim. In some organizations, victim mentality is rampant; it's become the cultural norm due to the complexity of the work, the demands of technology, customers, schedules, and the like. Victim mentality is what perpetuates a culture with no accountability. It's not because of the pressure—the volatile, uncertain, complex, and ambiguous, or "VUCA," world we live in. It's because no one wants to take ownership for anything.

Instead, we engage in blaming others, blaming schedules, blaming supply chains, blaming the CEO, blaming the time frame, blaming the team membership, blaming the stupid customers, blaming the UPS or delivery guy, whatever or whoever else we can find. Blaming is essentially saying, "I don't own what's going on. I have no control over what you think I'm supposed to have control over." That's the opposite of the truth. You and everyone who works with you, for you, and around you all have 100 percent control over the choices you make every day. No one is forcing any of you to do the job you're currently doing. You have chosen to show up for the job. Period. End of sentence.

You make choices about how you handle the pressure, the coworker, the schedule, the customer, the UPS guy, the volatility, the uncertainty, the change, and the ambiguity. Not everyone has great skills for handling all of these things. That's what coaching, training, and professional development are for. The point is that if you can name it, you can own it, and if you can own it, you can change it! You'll never get better at something when you're blaming someone or something else for it. If you choose victimhood and powerlessness over ownership and self-empowerment, you choose to remain weak—personally, professionally, and performancewise. Ownership is nothing if not power, the power to change, the power to make decisions, the power over circumstance, the power to self-actualize.

1:1 and Face-to-Face

Ownership is personal. It's not a group thing. You take it on yourself. While a team as a whole can be accountable for results, having an accountability conversation with a team is different than having an accountability conversation one to one. It's easy to hide in a group or think to yourself that it's not you but the others on the team who need to be more accountable for their performance. For that reason, I recommend you hold accountability conversations one to one as much of the time as possible.

Ownership comes in the full response to your comments. It's what you hear and what you see after you've stated the issues as described in Step 1 and the impacts as described in Step 3. You cannot hear the actual tone or see facial expressions and body language when you are not face-to-face with a person. When you're on the phone, you only get tone. When you email, you only get your own interpretation. Every step you take to move away from working face-to-face and one to one is a step further away from full accountability and clarity.

If you're working at distance, use online video chat tools. The phone is your second-best option. Never try to hold someone accountable in an email or text. No matter how much time and energy and thought you put into your words, you cannot guarantee how they will be received. You do not know if someone gets defensive as a result of reading your email, nor how much time and bourbon or general angst or malice occurred before they composed, then edited, then rewrote their response—or didn't respond at all! Emailing an attempt at accountability more often than not is ineffective. More than anything, it will read as a statement that you're just too busy to pick up the phone or walk down the hall or stand face-to-face and invest in some clarity by building your relationship with someone. Your conversations *are* your relationships. Emails are not conversations.

Tips for Engaging the Conversation

In Step 5, Engage the Conversation, remember these key points:

- **Leverage your script**. Your energy will change when you actually get eyeball to eyeball. Rely on your rehearsal and use the words you practiced regardless of how you're feeling. Have confidence in the practice you did. You will be surprised at how well it works.

- **If you get a confusing answer and are not clear on whether they've taken ownership, don't be afraid to get clear**. Just say, "I'm not clear on your response. You've said a lot of things. However, is this something you're taking ownership of, or are you telling me something different?" It's the question you most want answered. Get the answer.

- **Use the silence.** If you get nothing but silence, or maybe a deer-in-headlights expression, just wait. If you were clear in your opening statement and question, they've heard you. Wait for the response. The silence will be uncomfortable for you both. Resist the temptation to fill it—to make them comfortable and to make yourself comfortable. They will speak eventually. Your silence indicates that you are waiting and have nothing more to ask. Don't look away or busy yourself with other things while waiting. Wait patiently. Remain focused on them. It will feel like forever. That's fine. Embrace the awkwardness. There will be relief for both of you when they respond. However, you will lose your edge in the conversation should you break the silence first. Remember, breaking of the silence is a retreat, a choice to put comfort over clarity.

CHAPTER 11

Step 6: Build Solutions

Figure 24

OWNERSHIP FOR PERFORMANCE is as much about owning solutions as it is about owning mistakes. Improving performance is personal. When you give a person feedback and then proceed to tell them what they need to do to make it better, you are not gaining accountability. In fact, you are essentially taking it away. I'm not saying your intentions are bad. You think you are being helpful, saving time, and moving forward. You're moving on. But by telling people what they need to do, you are disallowing them an opportunity to problem solve for themselves and the organization. You're not really saving any time, and you're eliminating an opportunity for you to understand what your employees know or don't know and to learn how they think. Taking that opportunity goes directly to your ability to manage them more effectively or develop them properly.

Put another way, when you tell someone what they *need* to do, you choose your own happiness over theirs. That's not as harsh as it sounds, but it's very real—both neurochemically and philosophically. Let's start with the neurochemistry. Our brains love addiction. We crave the dopamine rush, and every time we feel we're right about something, we get a little hit. Every time you solve someone's performance problem by telling them what they *need* to do, you are giving yourself a little hit of dopamine. It's why we're all amused by the response we sometimes give to people when we tell them what we think they need to know and finish off the directive with "You're welcome." I'm getting high right now just writing about it.

You're welcome.

And now let's follow up with the philosophy. I'll reference again the book by Mark Manson called *The Subtle Art of Not Giving a F#ck*, where he explains beautifully:

> Happiness comes from solving problems ... Problems are
> a constant in life ... Problems never stop; they merely get

exchanged and/or upgraded. Happiness comes from solving problems … Happiness is therefore a form of action; it's an activity, not something that is passively bestowed upon you, not something that you magically discover in a top-ten article on Huffington Post or from any specific guru or teacher … Happiness is a constant work-in-progress because solving problems is a constant work-in-progress—the solutions of today's problems will lay in the foundation for tomorrow's problems and so on. True happiness comes when you find the problems you enjoy having and enjoy solving.[17]

Here's my favorite part: "*Whatever your problems are, the concept is the same: solve problems, be happy. Unfortunately, for many people, life doesn't feel that simple. That's because they fuck things up in at least one to two ways: (1) denial, (2) victim mentality.*"

See, it all comes full circle. Stop taking away the opportunity for someone to solve their own problems because you value your happiness over theirs. Take that first step in allowing them to develop; don't take away their opportunities for happiness. Of course, you know the answer. That's not the point. Let them discover on their own. And, of course, if they can't figure it out, let them in on how things can get done or be better. But create the space for growth in the moment.

Don't worry—you can still be happy. When you take the training wheels off and allow your employee to learn to master something on their own, you will have provided both support and confidence in their ability to learn. That's trust in action. Plus, now you can busy yourself with the pressing problems that belong to you. Are you feeling just a little hit of dopamine at the thought?

---

17   Mark Manson, *The Subtle Art of Not Giving a F#ck: A Counterintuitive Approach to Living a Good Life* (Harper Collins, 2016), 30–32.

Stop Leading and Facilitate Discovery

I talked about critical thinking earlier, but I'm bringing it back again here to remind you that it's an essential ingredient for success in your accountability conversation. When you get eyeball to eyeball and are entertaining the other person's response, it's important to stay grounded in the front of your head, in your prefrontal cortex, where all the strategy and trust work is done. That's to be distinguished from going to the back of your head, your amygdala or lizard brain, where all your distrust, fight, and protect work is done.

It's not enough to merely gain ownership for the issue; it's also essential to drive ownership for what will be done differently going forward. Open, probing questions kick that door ajar, opening the door to the other person's happiness. Using the open-question format gives you the advantage of finding yourself in a place of *discovery with* your employee as opposed to making *you need* statements where you are in a *power over* relationship. It also means you're listening, not protecting or controlling, and can easily pivot the conversation where it needs to go by virtue of the questions you ask. You guide the thinking, the responses. Your role here as a guide is itself an act of building trust.

So many managers rely on *leading* questions rather than open ones, which goes against the point of teaching people to think critically and become better problem solvers themselves. Those leading questions sound like: "Do you think it would have been better to ask Sally for her thoughts first before you spoke in front of the team?" or "Do you think you should have passed your copy by the communications department before putting the information on the website?" Duh! Of course. How was your dopamine hit? While you feel you may be getting them to think, you are very likely shutting down their capacity for problem-solving. What they may actually be thinking is: *Oh, for crying out loud! I get it! Quit humiliating me!* or *I don't need a lecture now, thank you.* If you tend to ask leading questions, that's probably because you have a lot of experience; you know you are right and like the dopamine hit. Sometimes those of us who are parents can have a hard time transitioning from a parental mindset of seeing our children as children instead of thinking teens and adults, which is to say we can end up seeing our employees as inexperienced and unknowing children. These tendencies can become patterns that are hard to break in our daily lives as managers. Sometimes managing can feel like parenting, but that should only strengthen my point about enabling others to think for themselves.

Critical thinking asks us to question openly before landing on an *answer* or solution. That sounds more like this: "In retrospect, how should you have handled the copy before posting it?" or "Based on the team's reaction, how do you think you should have dealt with Sally?" We learn so much faster through our failures. The key is to recognize those failures as opportunities to learn as opposed to the opportunity for you to be right.

When we ask the open question, we ask our direct reports, peers, and superiors how to think about it. In other words, we're looking to understand how they think. And from their response, we learn about what they know or need to learn or what motivates their actions. Gathering this information informs the next steps and makes for more suitable, accurate, and timely problem-solving overall.

Build Real Solutions

To get to true and effective accountability, the solutions need to be realistic. The goal, after all, is for others to own their own solutions, to solve their own problems. However, that doesn't mean you let them do any hairbrained thing they come up with. Sometimes a proposed solution is just not realistic. Help them assess: How realistic is their solution? Is it appropriate? Does it make sense within the realm of the performance problem, the culture, the history of their own abilities? You're looking for something attainable and sustainable by the other person. What is an achievable best effort for that person? Are they fully committed to it? If you can avoid it, do not give yourself something to do as well.

Engage your common sense here. Don't control the conversation, but don't let it get out of control either. You are responsible for maintaining the guardrails when it comes to your team's performance. Keep people on track, but don't drive the car. For example, if you're dealing with an issue of a critical report that is consistently delivered late and their solution is skipping a double check on accuracy or somehow skirting or diminishing a process, that's when you'd point out the guardrail. That might sound something like: "So if I understand your solution, you're thinking of skipping the step of double-checking in order to meet a deadline but potentially providing a report with errors? That may just shift the problem from one area to another. What else do you think you could do? What other ideas have you got?" Critical thinking is required for everyone when it comes to answering the important question: How do you do this better?

> Critical thinking is required for everyone when it comes to answering the important question: How do you do this better?

Take What You Can Get

In Step 5, I mentioned "partial ownership." This is when a person will only take ownership for some of the performance issue(s) you've set on the table and deny the rest for whatever reasons. This happens. Don't worry about it. *Deal with what they'll own first.* Build solutions for what they'll own. Later on, they might assume ownership for the rest by virtue of putting solutions into action. Or you may find it easier to gain ownership in the near future based on improved performance around what they do address. Or you may find you need to handle separately what hasn't been owned, or at least reevaluate it.

This strategy essentially asks you to put the relationship before the results. Allow the person the opportunity to deal with what they do own. You may be surprised by how easy gaining ownership over other things becomes.

Tips for Building Solutions

In Step 6, Build Solutions, keep these key points in mind:

- **Don't attempt to problem solve another person's performance**. Resist the urge to sell your employees on ideas you feel are best or will address performance issues quickly. You will undercut your efforts at achieving ownership, run the risk of losing real accountability, and diminish the self-reflection necessary for growth.

- **Don't attempt to rescue your underperformer**. This happens when you ask *leading* questions. Leading questions drive thinking in a direction that you prefer. Leading questions look for simple "yes" or "no" answers and undercut real accountability. Your preferences are irrelevant in terms of gaining ownership. Your discomfort over how long it may take for your employee or coworker to realize what their solution needs to be is secondary. Every once in a while, you may need to say, "Think about it, and get back to me." And that's okay.

CHAPTER 12

Listening Is Half the Conversation

Figure 25

A CRITICAL PART of Steps 5 and 6 is listening. Listening is more than half the conversation—especially on your end. Because accountability is an act of clarity, not only must you be clear on what your issue is; you must be clear on how the person responds to how you've identified the issue. The listening is about *hearing* what the person says in response to your issues, as well as *seeing* the nonverbal response. Nonverbals can be more important in that they will tell you more about how the other person is responding than the words they're using. A person may be saying, "Oh! I didn't realize that the deadlines were nonnegotiable! I'll certainly do better next time," while they're also leaning back with their arms crossed, frustration on their face, or their eyes aimed down at the floor or at the clock. The body will betray the language if the two are not aligned. Any response that's out of alignment—even when it sounds like ownership—is probably not, or at least not full ownership. Misalignment warrants additional clarity to see what exactly the person will own.

Likewise, if we're just on the phone, I cannot see the eye-rolling or mock-vomiting that could be taking place. Mind you, that's not what you should expect. In fact, if you suspect you're going to have that kind of reaction, then you've got bigger issues than accountability problems with that person. My point here is that observing nonverbal cues is an advantage in an accountability conversation because they contain valuable communication around whatever issue it is you're raising. If you can converse in person, do it. It's not a power play. It's a statement of respect. It's a statement of caring. When you show up in someone's office for an accountability conversation (or if they show up in yours, or you

> If you can converse in person, do it. It's not a power play. It's a statement of respect. It's a statement of caring.

both turn on the camera if you're meeting online), that's a statement that you both care enough to have the conversation in the first place. When you are put off, relegated to phone or email conversations, you and/or the issue are not important enough to make the time. Remember, how a person spends their time is a choice. "I'm sorry. I've been so busy" is an excuse for choosing to do something else rather than making time to address your issue.

What's the Emotional Response?

Listening is also a test of your emotional intelligence, your capacity to detect any overriding emotions driving the conversation. *Emotional intelligence* is a term brought into popularity in 1995 by Daniel Goleman with his book by the same name. As you can tell by its moniker, it's a skill set that also gives you an edge as a manager and leader. Goleman notes that EQ, given that it is "a different way of being smart, is a key to high performance at all levels, particularly for outstanding leadership. It's not your IQ; it's how you manage yourself and your relationships. There are four parts to the Emotional and Social Intelligence model: Self-Awareness, Self-Management, Social Awareness and Relationship Management."[18] I'll focus just on the first two here, Self-Awareness and Self-Management, as they are excellent for accountability work. Goleman defines Self-Awareness as "the ability to understand your own emotions and their effects on your performance. You know what you are feeling and why—and how it helps or hurts what you are trying to do." Your ability to maintain awareness of your own emotions also allows you space to be aware of the emotions of others. Goleman defines Self-Management

---

18   Daniel Goleman, Richard Boyatzis, Richard J. Davidson, Vanessa Druskat, and George Kohlreiser, *Emotional Self-Control: A Primer*, Building Blocks of Emotional Intelligence Series (More Than Sound, 2017), 7.

as "Emotional Self-Control … the ability to keep your disruptive emotions and impulses in check, to maintain your effectiveness under stressful or even hostile conditions. This doesn't mean suppressing your emotions. With Emotional Self-Control, you manage your impulses and emotions, staying clearheaded and calm." Emotional self-awareness and self-control help to explain why practicing the language and working with anticipated responses help when you're feeling any pressure in real time. Your brain loves a pattern. When you've run the drills in advance, you'll recognize any patterns that can aid you in executing an emotionally intelligent conversation and feedback experience.

Listening is a big part of detecting the emotional state of the person with whom you're talking. Can you detect anger or frustration or even apathy in some cases, or is the person coming across as emotionally neutral or rational? If you've heard rational ownership without any overriding emotional drive, then you're good to go on to solution building. However, if you detect even a little overriding emotional drive or complete lack of emotion (apathy), then chances are you're not clear yet.

Ownership in anger may only give you malicious compliance, which is the equivalent of getting someone's least good effort. This is why more clarity is in order. However, in this instance, you'll aim to get clarity about the anger or frustration (rather than clarity about what's been said).

Solutions built in anger are not real solutions; they are the path of least resistance. Taking this path generally leads to having the same conversation about the same thing at a later date. Pressing someone to move on, or simply ignoring any emotion, is the same as ignoring the response altogether or ignoring the person completely. It's like saying, "I have concerns about your presentation because you were unprepared for several questions that the customer brought up, and that impacts our credibility to deliver as promised. Now that I see how angry you are about what I just said, I don't want to talk to you anymore. So forget it. Never mind." How do you think the person feels then? Initially, they may have been just as concerned as you about the customer. But if you choose to ignore what the anger is about, you raise the risk that now they'll be concerned about their job maybe or about having to work for you. When they leave your office, they'll probably spend a lot of time reliving the conversation in their head and ginning up things they should have said that they didn't. And that activity can go on for them for days. Ignoring people turns out to be a great way to hijack productivity.

I'm not just arguing that emotions are as much a part of communication as language. In fact, I would venture to say that emotions are the primary communication for which we've had to develop language. An outstanding manager and leader consistently leverages their emotional intelligence as part of their day-to-day engagement with people because they know the emotional side is key for ongoing commitment and engagement in the organization. Not dealing with an emotional response to your issues around accountability is not an option. You will not be good at accountability if you're not leaning into your emotional intelligence as well. Listening for emotions doesn't make accountability more difficult; it actually

> An outstanding manager and leader consistently leverages their emotional intelligence as part of their day-to-day engagement with people because they know the emotional side is key for ongoing commitment and engagement in the organization.

makes it much easier. When you can deal with the emotions first, accountability comes faster.

Defensiveness

One of the biggest reasons we hold back on accountability is because of defensiveness—on either person's part. When we get defensive about something, it's generally because we are feeling attacked. Most of the time, that defensiveness is based more on perception than it is in reality. I assume that as a manager, you are not intentionally demeaning, criticizing, belittling, humiliating, or demoralizing the person who works for you—either verbally or in email. Instead, I'm referring here to the heightened negative emotional reaction people have to simple queries about the status of a project, impact of a presentation, or what happened in the meeting. I'm referring here to a response from the person hearing your question that seems out of proportion to the intention of the question.

Defensiveness can occur for people by just hearing someone who typically is looking for something from them—like a boss or team lead—coming down the hall. It's the result of a pattern for them. You might also have certain people whom you work with or are familiar with who trigger your defensiveness. We see this a lot in movies when adult children go home to visit parents and find themselves defensive about how they're living their lives, handling their marriages, or raising their children.

Generally, defensiveness is triggered by a feeling of either guilt or vulnerability. The guilty feeling may be coming from our understanding of something we did or didn't do. The vulnerable feeling is more about power dynamics, feeling powerless or judged in some way. It's an interesting dynamic in terms of holding people accountable. It can certainly get in the way because it essentially results in at least one person moving into an emotional state. As I mentioned before, it's a test of your emotional intelligence to recognize defensiveness when you hear it. When the other person has gone emotional, it's your job to see if you can bring them back to the rational in order to gain clarity, build solutions, and move forward.

Defensiveness can happen in either direction. The other person to whom you are speaking can respond defensively, or they can respond in a way that makes you get defensive (you perceive it as an attack). We are all susceptible to becoming defensive, and there may even be circumstances that drive more frequent defensive reactions—like intense business pressure with unrealistic deadlines or tight resources for getting the job done. Defensiveness can also arise as the result of physical triggers, such as poor diet and fatigue. Regardless of *why* someone goes defensive, hearing it and dealing with or de-escalating it is the most effective strategy for moving forward instead of going into a spiral.

Emotional Escalation and De-Escalation

When you are in the throes of an accountability conversation, anger and defensiveness can appear and derail the conversation unless you are listening for it and prepared to deal with it. Let's go back to the neurochemistry. What is happening for someone neurochemically when they are angry or defensive? I'll reference Judith E. Glaser's work here again: they begin releasing cortisol and swimming in the cortisol-norepinephrine-testosterone cocktail or "feel bad conversation." Their vision narrows. Their hearing becomes diminished. They enter *fight and protect* mode. Their lizard brain has kicked into gear.

YOUR BRAIN ON ACCOUNTABILITY

CONDITIONAL TRUST
Neocortex and Limbic/Mid Brain Activation

WHAT AM I HEARING?
HOW IS THAT MAKING ME FEEL?
WHAT'S MY EXPERIENCE
WITH THIS ISSUE AND
THIS PERSON?

HIGH TRUST
Prefrontal Cortex/Executive Brain Activation

HOW CAN I
SOLVE THIS
AND DO BETTER?

LOW TRUST
Amygdala/Lizard Brain Activation

AM I SAFE?
DO I BELONG?
RUN/FIGHT/IGNORE?

SELF PROTECTION,
DENIAL & DEFENSIVENESS

PARTNERSHIP/RELATIONSHIP
AND OWNERSHIP

*All or parts of the content presented here are adapted from **Conversational Intelligence**® and the work of Judith E. Glaser.*

Figure 11

There are two essential questions we ask ourselves when confronted with any situation that requires us to engage: "Am I safe or not safe?" and "Do I belong, or do I not belong?" When a person is confronted by feedback about how they've performed, both of these questions are in play at the beginning of the conversation. You have zero control over that. The need to answer those questions is hardwired in our brains; that need is how we survive. The key is to recognize anger and defensiveness and deal with them. And by "deal with them," I mean name it, acknowledge it, and de-escalate the intensity. Escalation, like defensiveness, can happen very easily; a lot of times it can feel like it comes out of nowhere. You may ask a simple question, like "How are your sales numbers looking this month?" And you'll get an intense or emotionally laden response like, "The only time you ever talk to me is when you want to know my numbers!" That response may be even more likely if the person you are asking is underperforming on sales, and you intend to hold them accountable for the number they've committed to closing.

De-escalating the intensity of these emotional responses means getting the other person out of their lizard brain or amygdala hijack by neurochemically upregulating them. Think of it like negotiating a hostage situation or talking someone off the proverbial ledge. The best way to handle this is to talk about your intention: "My intention is not to attack you ..." This lets the other person know how they are being perceived as well as encourages the neurochemical shift out of the back of the head into a place of conditional trust. Continue the thought with a question shift into curiosity: "I am just trying to understand where things stand. And I'm concerned you may need help or support, but I'm not clear on that. Can you share with me where things stand to see if there's a possible solution to get you where you wanted to be?"

I realize the conversation may not end there. The other person may continue to feel attacked. However, that's the practice. If I were coaching you through this scenario, I would press you to explore more what-ifs to cover as much as possible of what you could expect. The important thing is to remember to deal with another person's heightened, negative emotional state. Otherwise, they are likely to feel ignored, or, as can happen in some cases, you can become defensive based on the defensive response they've given you. I'm sure you can imagine how unproductive it would be were you to end up feeling attacked (either guilty or vulnerable) and as a result entering *fight and protect* mode. You'll end up swimming in the cortisol cocktail. You'll stop listening effectively, and any hope of coming to a clear and solid resolution around the accountability issue you are dealing with will be lost. This is also why you never ever deal with accountability problems when you are angry. For some, it takes way more than merely counting to ten before opening your mouth. Escalation can happen in seconds—you'll remember that, neurochemically, that's something like 0.07 seconds. Verbally, that could be three sentences.

Consider the following example:

"Hey, Brianna, where are you on that month-end report?"

"Oh, for crying out loud, Ted, how many times are you gonna ask me about that thing?"

"As many times as I want to, Brianna. I'm your boss. Maybe you should try giving me an answer."

Now, let's track the emotional states:

LANGUAGE	EMOTIONAL STATE
Hey, Brianna, where are you on that month-end report?	Rational—Rational (Best Case)
Oh, for crying out loud, Ted, how many times are you gonna ask me about that thing?	Rational—Emotional (Escalation)
As many times as I want to, Brianna. I'm your boss. Maybe you should try giving me an answer.	Emotional—Emotional (Fight)

The best conversations around ownership are rational. However, as soon as one person goes emotional, everything can change for the worse unless you de-escalate. To do that, you have to stop the conversation, change the language, and change the focus to address the emotional state.

Let's consider how a different version might proceed:

"Hey, Brianna, where are you on that month-end report?"

"Oh, for crying out loud, Ted, how many times are you gonna ask me about that thing? I'm workin' on it!"

"Okay, Brianna. Hang on, let's stop here for a second.… My intention in asking you is based on my own scheduling availability. I'm coming up on a lot of premeeting one-on-ones that I have to do. I'm asking you now because I want to make sure we've got time to meet and go over the details before we present it to the board."

"Oh … I didn't realize you were booked up so tight before the meeting. Let me see what I can do to get a copy to you by the end of the week. Have you got thirty minutes to meet next week and go over it? I work better under deadline pressure anyway."

Let's track the emotional states in this version:

LANGUAGE	EMOTIONAL STATE
Hey, Brianna, where are you on that month-end report?	Rational–Rational (Best Case)
Oh, for crying out loud, Ted, how many times are you gonna ask me about that thing?	Rational–Emotional (Escalation)

Okay, Brianna. Hang on, let's stop here for a second.... My intention in asking you is based on my own scheduling availability. I'm coming up on a lot of premeeting one-on-ones that I have to do. I'm asking you now because I want to make sure we've got time to meet and go over the details before we present it to the board.	Rational–Emotional (De-escalation)
Oh ... I didn't realize you were booked up so tight before the meeting. Let me see what I can do to get a copy to you by the end of the week. Have you got thirty minutes to meet next week and go over it? I work better under deadline pressure anyway.	Rational–Rational (Ownership/Solution)

Not every conversation will escalate in three sentences or resolve in four sentences, but many of them can and do. In my coaching work, I've seen just how frequently people are continually surprised by how fast you can de-escalate and resolve.

The Moment of Ownership: Acceptance versus Rejection

Your ability to listen to and know the difference between taking ownership and denying ownership affects your ability to move the conversation in the most productive direction while staying focused on the issue at hand. This is the point in the conversation you've been waiting for: the moment of acknowledgment, the taking of responsibility for actions, decisions, and results that will allow you to move forward into solution building, progress, and hopefully even development. Oddly enough, this is the point where many managers lose the plot and end up having a conversation about something completely different than expected. So let's look at both acceptance and rejection to think about how your listening skills can help you decide how to move the conversation to conclusion.

Acceptance

The frequency with which acceptance takes place can be a sign of the extent to which a workplace has got a culture of accountability. If you currently work in such a culture, you'll recognize that you get acceptance more often than not because it's the norm. If you don't work in a culture of accountability, you'll get a lot of conditional language that sounds like "I own this, however …" or "Absolutely we missed the deadline, but …" or "I can appreciate your perspective on the project, yet …." Now, I'm not saying that sentences like these can't be valid or true. But they are also deflections, which ultimately is a form of denial. The important thing is to listen fully so that you can identify what exactly is being owned.

Acceptance starts out like all the examples we just reviewed. The difference is that it also finishes there:

Manager: "Vicki, I want to talk to you about missing the deadline on this last report. The project team had to reschedule an entire day of meetings as a result because they did not have the information to make decisions. Talk to me about that."

Vicki: "You're absolutely right. I missed it by two days. I feel terrible and have given thought as to how to do things differently. I made some bad decisions prioritizing my time. I appreciate the feedback. I have apologized to the team. Is there something else I could do to make it right?"

That's ownership. But Vicki might confuse you and respond like this instead:

Vicki: "You're absolutely right. I was forced to miss the deadline by two days. I was waiting on some updates and thought I should get some other work done while waiting. The team has too many priorities. And I'm sure I'm not the only one."

If Vicki talks around the issue before landing on ownership or rounds onto ownership somewhere in the middle of her story of messing up and how she's going to fix it, then it's on you to ask for clarity. Don't stay confused. If you think she's taken ownership, confirm that with her:

Manager: "So based on everything you've just told me and explained, you're taking ownership for missing the deadline and are prepared to meet it next time? I just want to be clear."

Here, resolution comes through owning the performance result as well as preempting solution building. However, don't expect that all the time. You may just get: "You're absolutely right. I missed it by two days, and I feel terrible." At which point you'll then want to move into Step 6: Facilitating Solutions.

Here's another example of an ownership conversation:

Manager: "Chris, my expectation is that you're here every day at 8:00 a.m. to begin work. I'm concerned because you consistently choose to show up between twenty and forty minutes late. Talk to me about that."

Chris: "Ugh … I know I do. I'm sorry. I really need to be here on time … I know."

This example also demonstrates straight-up ownership and allows you to move into Facilitating Solutions. That next step might sound like this:

Manager: "Yeah, I know you know. What I'm really interested in speaking to you about is how you think you'd like to handle it."

You'll notice that there's no reference to "need" (e.g., "You need to get up earlier"). The best solutions are also owned by the person who must engage them.

Rejection

Now let's talk about rejection—also known as denial of a performance issue. Denial is the most common response in an accountability conversation, and it can create a slippery slope. It's important that you learn to recognize it and understand clearly what to do when you encounter it in accountability conversations.

Because we humans don't like to look bad or create conflict, we often look for ways to distance or deflect the impact on ourselves through a range of specific tactics. We've got three primary tactics of denial: run, fight, and ignore.

Run

Running is the form of denial of ownership that includes behaviors like avoidance, crying, self-attack, and putting off. Avoidance is literally not dealing with a performance issue, and avoidance behaviors include not responding to emails, not showing up for meetings, not answering calls, or sending specific callers to voice mail and then not responding to the voice mail. Crying is obviously an emotional response, which can be tricky to deal with for both men and women, but especially men. Crying can be triggered by any number of things, including insecurity (a form of vulnerability), oversensitivity (intense feelings), and fatigue (tiredness combined with a sense of being overwhelmed).

Here's the thing: it's not important to know *why* someone is crying. What's important is to recognize crying in this instance as an emotional response and a form of denial. Responding to it requires recognition of the emotion, patience and empathy, and not letting the other person off the hook. Instead, responding is about a compassionate, supportive, and clear approach in continuing the conversation, creating space and giving pause while the person recenters themself to stay in the conversation. Crying may make you uncomfortable and knock you off-center, but that just means it's something you'll need to practice responding to.

Crying is designed to trigger us biologically. That's okay. Be aware of when you are triggered—use your emotional intelligence—and consider how best to respond. I've already mentioned that shutting down the conversation is the worst course of action because the emotions are also part of the conversation. When you shut the conversation down, even under the guise of a claim like "perhaps this isn't a good time to have this conversation," you're essentially choosing to ignore this person for the time being because you're uncomfortable with their response. That's a weak response on your part, and you know it. Some managers even get irritated when employees cry. While you may be irritated because you're thinking, *What am I supposed to do with that?* your irritation is probably more to do with the fact you're completely unprepared for how to handle it when an employee cries in response to your feedback. A better response to crying is to empathize with the emotional response. Offer up a box of tissues. Go to intention. "My intention was not to make you cry. Take a moment to gather your thoughts." Then continue when you feel they've recentered, or make a statement to that effect.

Self-attack is a behavior that includes self-admonishing responses like: "I know; I suck at that, and I don't know if I'm ever going to get it right" or "My bad!" or "I'm a complete failure. This obviously isn't the job for me." As you can see, there are varying levels from not-so-serious to actual and deep self-doubt. In any case, it's not important that you dig into the self-deprecation, as that puts you into territory you are most likely not credentialed to deal with. In an account-ability conversation, self-attack is a form of denial, so take it as that, and then move the conversation from there. If the self-deprecation is really a form of self-doubt, then it will come up again when you get to solution building, and you can address it there as either a skill deficit or behavioral issue.

Putting off or delaying is another form of running from ownership. Delaying is the hope that if you wait a little longer, the issue will either go away or won't be as important. Putting off is essentially a misguided self-protecting behavior that more often aggravates and escalates performance issues than mitigates or reduces them. When you have given a person feedback and are looking for them to take ownership, and their response is to put off or delay further conversation until a later time (for whatever reason), that's when you should recognize denial.

Putting off can seem very convincing and will sound something like: "I hear what you're saying, and I don't want to diminish the importance of that. However, I'd like to put a pin in this until next week when I've got additional information from my team, and I can respond to you with a clearer and better answer," or "I know this is very important. But I need a little time to get my head together to respond intelligently. Can we set up some time next week?" Remember, you're most likely bringing up the situation because something about timeli-ness is off track—work is behind, the deadline has passed, or there is some urgency to speaking about the issue now. Stay in the moment. A potential response could sound something like: "Yes. I understand you feel unprepared; that is exactly the concern I have. It's important we speak now. Let's take a few minutes."

Fight

Fighting as a form of denial of ownership shows up in behaviors like arguing, blaming, yelling, or actual physical fighting (which in the workplace is pretty rare but can happen under intense pressure and extreme working conditions). Fighting is the most common form of denial you'll experience when you are in an accountability conversation, and that's because it involves arguing and blaming, which are the most common responses to poor performance or not meeting expectations. I may already have hinted that blaming is the number one response: "It's not really my fault" will be combined with the appropriate finger-pointing to other people, systems, processes, or events that conspired to bring on the disappointing results. Remember, although bad things can happen that are out of our control, that is not the point. You are having an accountability conversation to gain clarity around ownership and expectations. While bad things may have occurred that helped diminish or even train-wreck a business result, the questions you're ultimately trying to answer are "How did you handle all those challenges?" or "Did you even attempt to handle those challenges?" and, most important, "Do you understand those challenges were yours to handle appropriately?"

Many forms of blaming are relationship-driven, which is to say they take this form: "I couldn't deliver my result because a person with whom I work set me up to fail; they did not get me what I needed so that I could get my work done." As managers, our knee-jerk, problem-solving reaction is to move into a line of questions about what's going on there: "Do I need to get your coworker in here so the two of you can sort this out?" Or if this issue is across organizational divisions, the knee-jerk managerial question might be "Do I need to get in touch with this guy's boss (my peer) to let him know that his employee is not cooperating with my team?" If you think about this in terms of familial relations, this sort of response is very much akin to a tactic I like to call "blame your sibling and wait until your father gets home." The key here is to understand that blaming, regardless of the technique and how compelling the reason, is still a form of denial and should be heard as such. In response, you should move the accountability conversation forward from there and not into problem solving the blame. There is no follow-up question here. Do not engage this response conversationally. Treat it as denial of ownership.

Here's another nugget to consider as you ponder how often your employees blame others in the organization regardless of their position. If the person they are blaming works with your employee to deliver a business result, then the expectation should also be to have positive and productive working relationships within and across the organization at all times. That's to say: you are not the parent, and it's not your job to make sure all the kids get along. You are a working professional, managing other working professionals who should all understand and know how to forge productive working relationships regardless of where in an organization those relationships are taking place. Those professionals should know how to address the key relationship that should be maintained to deliver expected business results.

If you're rolling your eyes after reading this, thinking, *Oh yeah, good luck with that! There are so many people who can't get along*, let me say: yes. But if you don't expect them to get along and if you don't hold them to that expectation, you're the one who allows the behavior to continue, and that's on you. Culture is everyone's job.

A follow-up nugget: When, as the manager, you insert yourself into your employees' work relationships (even with the best intention to resolve issues), you are usurping the authority of each person's ability to build and maintain their own relationships. To the extent that you do that, you can diminish the value of each person in the other person's view. Based on the issue and how the finger-pointing went down, when you step into the fray, the trust can end up broken between those people.

Trust is the *number one* ingredient for thriving relationships of any kind. In their book, *The Trusted Advisor Fieldbook: A Comprehensive Toolkit for Leading with Trust*, Charles H. Green and Andrea P. Howe discuss a tactical, business understanding of trust. They describe trust as an exchange: one person trusts, and the other person is trusted, which is to say that trust is created in interactions. You are evaluated by the quality of what you say, how others describe what you do, whether or not people feel comfortable sharing certain information with you, and whether or not they feel you are prepared to put their interests above your own. Inserting yourself, or "handling the situation," as you may want to say to validate your actions, puts trust at risk every time. You effectively diminish trust when you move to manage out of what is perceived as self-interest. Lack of trust is the number one culture killer, and your behavior can be part of the reason trust is lacking organizationally. This is why accountability for more than just a result carries so much cultural potency.

Accountability is never just about the result. In fact, it's mostly about *how* you got the result.

Ignore

Ignoring includes behaviors like minimizing and intellectualizing. A minimizing response in an accountability conversation sounds like,

"I hear what you're saying. Can we put a pin in this? I know you're looking for good numbers this month, and I'm minutes from a client call. Can I catch up with you on this later?" Sometimes the response can be much shorter and sharper and make you feel like an idiot for even bringing something up to begin with. In fact, it could almost be a power play, more of a challenge. Like bucks in the wild, someone might challenge you, "Look how big my antlers are!" without actually locking horns, so to speak.

Intellectualizing is more about attempting to reframe a situation to avoid ownership and accountability. Intellectualizing might sound like, "I think I understand what you're saying … however, I'm wondering why it is that our team seems to be getting the short end of the stick on this process. It seems to me that the funding considerations are imbalanced and that we're stuck with a much larger proportion of the responsibilities without the appropriate resources to really be effective. In my view, we should really be examining how the process is working." This sort of response could potentially send a manager into their lizard brain (amygdala hijack), especially if they're the person who developed the process or who may now feel suckered by someone else who did. Either way, if you start focusing on the process, then you've lost the point of the accountability conversation altogether. Here, again, resist the temptation to engage in the reframe. Recognize that what you've heard is denial, and respond to it as such.

You'll get denial most of the time when you attempt accountability, until you start practicing it with consistency. All it takes is a few conversations where you no longer dive into issues around denial for your employees to figure out that those responses no longer hold water.

Denial Is a Diversion

All detail-giving—of whatever kind—is just a diversion from accepting responsibility and taking ownership for outcomes. Period. End of sentence.

When you have an accountability conversation, you're setting the table with an issue. You've thought about exactly what the issue is and how it's impacting you and the organization. Then, you're sliding that issue across the table to the other person because you'd like them to pick it up and deal with it. Denial is the enticing-looking bowl of plastic fruit someone else sets on the table in response to the issue you've laid out. See the plastic fruit. Do not take a bite! It's a bowl of denial. When you take the plastic fruit into your hand, you're taking up whatever diversion the other person has thrown out there. Not only will you leave the table unsatisfied, but you may also leave feeling worse in that you've now discovered a whole host of other issues you may have not known about and now feel responsible for dealing with. Those little plastic bits you've digested are making your tummy hurt! Save yourself the indigestion and heartache. Don't eat the fruit! Instead, see the label on the fruit that says: "flavors of denial."

What do you do with the plastic fruit? You see it for what it is, and you address it as such. You seek clarity. You aim for critical thinking. You do both at the same time by asking a clarifying question that will sound something like, "I hear everything you just said. However, what I'm really hearing is that you're not taking any responsibility for <fill in the blank>. Is that what you're telling me?" This is a simple question that keeps the conversation on track and focused on the issue that you've presented. It's important, too, that this question comes from a place of clarity and curiosity. Any tone other than that, and you can end up sounding like you're making a malicious accusation—that's not what you want at all.

Listening with Empathy and Compassion

When you are empathetic, you galvanize feelings of understanding, feelings of mutuality. You make it safe for you and the other person. In the case of accountability conversations, empathy is about being and staying in the feeling of discovery and learning. To be clear, it's *not* about feeling how the other person is feeling about the feedback you are providing. After reviewing all the modes of denial, you can understand why you don't want to feel how the other person may be feeling. You want to be present with that person—a stance that allows you to recognize denial and to move into clarifying questions, and clarity itself, much more easily.

Empathy allows you to successfully guide the mood. When you are not attacking or accusing or angry about results, when you are instead concerned and curious, your mood is more contagious. If you've been enjoying the neurochemical explanations, how you set the table and how you respond to what the other person says and offers can positively trigger their mirror neurons. They'll do as you do. And if you need a quick primer on the neurochemistry, recall that in 1999, researchers led by Giacomo Rizzolatti discovered that our brain has unique neurons, called mirror neurons, that give us insight into what others feel, think, and intend. When we create space to listen more deeply (not just to respond), we turn off our tendency to judge and can create more connection with others. When our mirror neurons are activated, we have more empathy. When we are fearful, that power to connect is switched off, and so is our sensitivity to others' perspectives.

Within the flow of the conversation, you'll move from empathy to compassion. That means you'll move from mutuality—a feeling of shared discovery—into a feeling of understanding and assistance. Compassion creates space for understanding and willingness to help the other person build solutions that will work effectively going forward.

Tips for Listening

As you practice developing your capacity to listen, keep the following points in mind:

- **It's helpful if you can approach the conversation as an opportunity to connect with the other person.** An accountability conversation is about clarity, so creating space for understanding in addition to ownership is the goal. Leverage human biology—our need to connect—to make the conversation easier for both you and the person you are holding accountable.

- **It's unwise to hold an accountability conversation when you are angry, because your emotional state is triggered.** You'll be functioning using your lizard brain and won't be able to access trust, empathy, or strategy. The only thing you'll succeed at is communicating your anger. You might gain complacency. You might feel better having gotten things off your chest. Everything else in the relationship will be put at risk.

- **There is a distinction to be drawn between being supportive and asking, "What can I do to help?"** Asking what you can do to help is an easy sentence for many managers, and many use it in the context of an accountability conversation to soften their own discomfort around gaining ownership and accountability. It's a couching question more than anything else. It can sound like, "Cindy, as you know, the report on project status is critical for the team meeting. However, you're not getting it done in a timely manner. What can I do to help?" When a manager sets the table in this way, they have essentially taken away the ownership at the last moment. They've put the issue out there and then usurped responsibility by taking back ownership of a potential solution. This move muddies the waters, even if the manager's earnest intent is to help. Don't ask how you can help before you've gained ownership. Once the other person has taken ownership, once a solution is agreed upon, then and only then should you ask, "Is there anything you are expecting from me?" or "What, if anything, would help you in your efforts?" And even then, only ask that if you think it's necessary.

PART III
Time Shift

EXPAND YOUR THINKING

GETTING TO "YES, AND..."

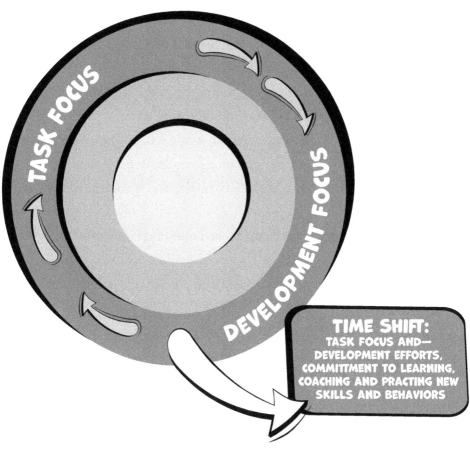

Figure 26

NOW THAT YOU'VE GOT AN UNDERSTANDING of the Six Ownership Steps and how to begin your practice, you might be thinking, *That's great; I'm good to go.* Yes and no. Yes, you're ready to get going. No, you're not yet finished. The final part of this book is all about the "now what?" of accountability. For some smaller, less complex issues, you may very well be good to go. You might be fine having created clarity and achieved ownership. However, if nothing changes, you don't really have accountability, especially when it comes to issues that demand behavior modification or need specific skills developed. More critically, additional support for change is necessary when it comes to deeper performance issues stemming from conflicts. Full accountability is achieved when there is ownership *for what happens next.*

Stopping the conversation at the point of clear ownership of the performance issue itself is the crux of why accountability and feedback become conflated and ineffective. From a manager's perspective, you have done the work of holding a person accountable, and it's implied that things should change or get back on track. The problem is that this is where employees are left hanging. They know they've done it wrong, missed the mark, failed the team, or what have you. You may be ready to move on. Your employee may not be. Your employee may simply now be clear around the performance issue, yet may still be feeling bad or ashamed, or at a very minimum painfully aware of their shortcomings. High-performing managers, the kind we all deserve and want to be, are the ones who consistently show up for the next part—supporting the development or change they've just discussed.

In Part I, I shared the results of studies conducted to see how well managers are taking up coaching efforts within organizations. You'll recall that part of the reason managers were not coaching was because they claimed not to "have time" to coach. I also said that how you spend your time is a choice. Achieving the last part of accountability, the ownership for change and improvement, is an important part of overall success. That is why this last shift is about time. Development requires a commitment to making better choices.

How much time is involved? That time commitment will vary both for you and for your employee. However, once you've got accountability, you're more likely to also have willingness. It's that willingness that both creates time and saves time. Remember the Performance Drivers & Choice Points diagram, which speaks directly to the amount of time you can expect to spend with employees building performance solutions and improvements. The time commitment you can expect to spend holding peers accountable should be limited mostly to your effort preparing and engaging them in the accountability conversation. The same goes for up-line conversations. Your prep and rehearsal may be the bulk of your time in those instances.

Finally, we must also consider what happens when you gain no ownership, when after your best effort to achieve clarity, your employee still feels as though they have no control to do what's expected or does not see their part in a performance problem. When your employee chooses to stand in victimhood or blame, or in denial of the choices they have and can make, you must close out with consequences. That choice is all yours. Consequences are the corollary effect that must be put into play on your part to achieve real accountability. Without them, accountability is just an idea without teeth.

CHAPTER 13

Managing Consequences

Figure 27

THERE IS NO ACCOUNTABILITY without consequences. As I said earlier, consequences are the ugly twin of accountability. You cannot have one without the other. We all prefer not to have to *go there*. However, if we cannot *go there*, we cannot have full accountability.

We tend to think of a consequence as punishment, but a consequence is simply the result or effect of actions or inaction or a condition. A punishment is the infliction or imposition of a penalty as retribution for an offense. I make this distinction here to illustrate that although there is a common resistance among managers when it comes to consequences for underperformance, consequences are simply corollary ramifications that impact the business, the team, work relationships, trust, and the like.

There are also results and effects when a person chooses to blame others, to argue, and to deny responsibility when given the opportunity to think deeply and self-reflect. And there are consequences when a person chooses to stand in the moment, openly, with courage, seeing themselves as they've been experienced by others, and to pursue growth and opportunities for positive change. As managers and leaders, we hold people accountable because we want results, but we also want strong performers, learning, and growth, and we want to tap into change that yields improvement. As professionals in a work environment, we also expect that we work with other professionals who want the same things in terms of personal growth, change, and development.

When someone denies accountability, they say "no" to change. They say "no" to growth. They say "no" to seeing themselves and taking the opportunity to be better. When "no" is the answer, managers and leaders must examine whether this is the right person for the role, the job, the project, or the team. So we turn to consequences to examine what leverage we have available to compel a change of perspective, a change of heart, better and more authentic self-reflection, and ultimately the examination of previous choices in the hope that this will turn toward the better for all concerned. That's really all a consequence is meant to do. The pain or distress that we associate with consequences comes from the recognition that we must stand in the moment regardless. If you are driving accountability, the moment of ownership never goes away. You either face it head-on and stand in your ownership at the outset, or you stand in the moment later within the framework of consequences. It comes either way.

Consequences have a bad rap because of the unevenness with which they are chosen. Consequences can end up *outweighing* the condition, the choices, the impacts of the results. This is why it's important to be thoughtful about consequences. Don't jump into consequences immediately (and certainly not in anger), because the emotional drive will cause that lack of balance and show up as a demonstration of power rather than as an opportunity to reevaluate, reframe, and refocus for the better.

When you find yourself in a position to propose a consequence, it must be proportionate to the issue at hand. There must be a balance between the issue and the consequence. The severity of consequences should escalate relative to the severity of the issues.

> **When you find yourself in a position to propose a consequence, it must be proportionate to the issue at hand.**

Proportional and Timely

A conversation about consequences is an entirely separate conversation. It's more effective to create space between acknowledging a lack of ownership for results or performance issues on the one hand and engaging consequences on the other. That said, the conversation about consequences must also be timely. Just like feedback, it should come on the heels of the conversation where you learned that your person was not going to accept ownership. Take a day or two to reflect on the appropriate consequences and then have that conversation.

Don't go beyond that time frame unless you've got to coordinate with human resources to bring them into the conversation. If you are coordinating with human resources, then let the other person know that you're scheduling time to follow up and that it may be longer than two days because you're coordinating a time when human resources can be present. This knowledge adds weight. It also creates space for a person who is reluctant to take ownership to do so before consequences can be introduced. However, let me be very clear on this point: *I am not suggesting you leverage the presence of human resources as a way to gain ownership with reluctant people.* That's a power play to speed things up, demonstrate authority, or avoid taking the time to think things through on your own. It creates a lack of balance and shows you to be less than invested in the relationships you have with your direct reports.

Impactful for the Individual

In considering consequences for a performance issue, it's important to think about unintended consequences for yourself and everyone else who could be potentially impacted. Remember back in chapter 2 when we considered the ways that parents using time-out as a consequence for their kids' bad behavior end up putting themselves in time-out along with the kids. If possible, don't present consequences that you will also have to endure as a manager or that your other employees will have to endure. Only if it's a team issue—an all-for-one-and-one-for-all behavior—should there be a team consequence.

Necessary for Learning

There are all kinds of different people with all kinds of different learning styles. Sometimes people have to endure consequences to understand the lesson. It's just a fact. If you are timid or reluctant to deal in consequences, you are denying these learners the opportunity to improve. The whole thing about accountability is it holds a standard; it's there to ensure that *better* is a real thing. Most people want to do a good job. It's your job as a manager and leader to create the opportunity for that to happen, and sometimes consequences are a means of getting the job done. So be sure to match your intention with consequences. If you intend consequences to drive growth as opposed to penalize or as retribution, you'll do a far better job gaining ownership and growth; you'll achieve *better* in the end.

Consult on Your Judgment

When considering what the consequences should be, don't be afraid to consult a mentor, peer, manager, or your human resources business partner. Not every consequence is about getting written up or having a Performance Improvement Plan officially drawn up and made part of someone's employment record. Sometimes a consequence is simply being removed from a project either temporarily or permanently (whichever you judge proportionate). Sometimes it might involve denying visibility or access by removing the person from the presentation or meeting. Some consequences may be as simple as temporarily adjusting your expectations. For example, if you're dealing with deadline issues on a monthly report, adjust the expectation to weekly until you feel the work is getting done. These consequences send clear messages about what may happen if the other person is not willing to own up to their responsibilities.

Tips for Managing Consequences

As you consider whether the consequences are proportionate to the issue, keep in mind the following points:

- **There is a fundamental shift in a working relationship when you have to deal with consequences.** Recognize that the change in your level of trust—the degree of reliability and transparency with this person—may now be and feel different. This is not a time to cut people off, be resentful, or create distance. Your success in selecting consequences with impact, consequences that create a change, is tied to your success in maintaining a people-positive attitude throughout the duration of a consequence.

- **The time of doling out a consequence is also a time for self-reflection on your part.** Review your part of the management relationship. Were you consistently clear in your expectations? Did you appropriately delegate? Might you have deep-ended somebody, setting them up to fail in ways you did not anticipate? Are you making an example of someone? Are you punishing a *fall guy* for something you cannot own up to?

- **Most people want to do a good job.** It's only the actively disengaged who summon consequences, often because they don't know what else to do about their situation.

CHAPTER 14

Owning Development

How Accountability Drives Change and Improvement

Figure 28

AT THE VERY START of this book, I wrote about the difference between managing for performance and coaching for development. I did that to offer some clarity, especially given that many organizations use the word *coaching* interchangeably with the word *feedback* and with the corresponding expectation that a feedback conversation will culminate in improved performance. This is not always the case. In fact, it is rarely the case when it comes to complex performance problems like broken relationships among teammates, or low self-awareness and self-insight, or lack of critical-thinking skills. These are things that will take both knowledge and practice to develop and master.

I am fond of saying that performance can change in a single conversation. I believe this is true—not because a person will magically master a skill within fifteen minutes and do their job better right then and there, but because once a person acknowledges the choices they have made, they take control of their own growth. They recognize that there is relief in taking responsibility, and there is power to make change, to be and to do better. What's even more exciting is the feeling of support the other person gets from an accountability conversation done well, the sense that it's okay. Don't underestimate this.

It's the feeling that you want to have as well. This is the moment of trust, of courage, and of vulnerability that you both experience together, and that is what bonds you in the relationship and what keeps you moving forward together. That feeling, that moment, is a result of how well you engage in the conversation. It's your prepared state, your focus on exactly what's at issue, and the absence of judgment on your part that produces the feeling of support and caring. As you well know by now, it's also the neurochemistry of dopamine, serotonin, and oxytocin that drives solution building and allows a person to shift perspective and see things a new way. The relief comes because the release of cortisol stops as the stress of the unknown or the fear of being judged disappears. The story that was being told internally is not true, and the new story emerges—the story of learning and change.

Slide Right into Coaching

Once you've got ownership and agreement, and the conversation feels like the next question is "now what?" that's your cue. That's the time to shift into a coaching mindset. Instead of asking "How can I help?" ask, "How can I support you?" Once you're at the point of ownership for the issue, you're also at the point of ownership for solutions. Ask yourself: "How do I support this person's ability to improve?" "What is my role here now?" "Is this an opportunity for coaching?"

Three Simple Options

The best part of arriving at this point is that you've only got three options:

1. You train them up on a skill or accelerate the level of a skill (close a skills gap),

2. You coach them to modify a behavior, or

3. You counsel them on how things stand (restating and clarifying expectations and asking for a different choice going forward).

Let's revisit the Performance Drivers & Choice Points model and how we use this to analyze our next steps in driving accountability. This time, we're not *managing* performance; instead, we're improving performance and supporting our employees through the next steps for growth and change.

Earlier, when I introduced the Performance Drivers & Choice Points model (see figure 29), we used it as a tool for analyzing the performance choices the other person is making. It served as the starting point for how we frame the accountability conversation. Now, we're using that same framework to aid in our approach in coaching. Based on how the other person responded in our S.O.S. Conversation, we know where the choice point is. That means we know now whether we are to take up a coaching role or a counseling role. If counseling is the right next step, you may need to ask for additional support from human resources, business partners, or other employee assistance program advocates.

Let's revisit the diagram with the added understanding of how the choice point positions you to engage employee growth and development. As you can see, there's a hard line at the choice point between skills and attitude. That hard line is an indication of where your shift in approach lives. Everything to the left (poor choices around skills or poor choices around behaviors) represents an opportunity for you to either coach or train the employee. Everything to the right (choices around attitude and beliefs and values) represents an opportunity for you to counsel the employee.

PERFORMANCE DRIVERS & CHOICE POINTS™

WHAT ARE YOU COACHING?

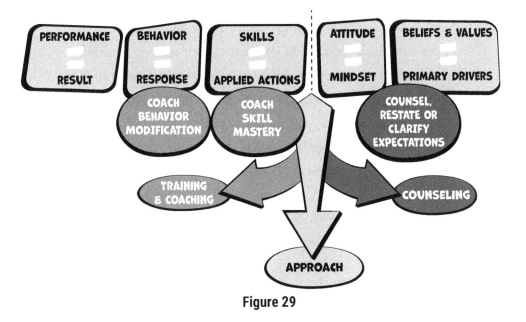

Figure 29

Coaching Is a Deeper Level of the Management Relationship

I want you to be clear about the nature of coaching and the desire and commitment it takes to be a successful coach in addition to being a successful manager. Your work as a *coach* positions the other person as the *learner*. That differs from other work relationships.

In today's highly competitive global marketplace, coaching is a coveted skill because it is the most-valued component in generating greater productivity through people. High people productivity is a business imperative for any organization, so effective coaching is a key competency for you to achieve your desired levels of productivity as a manager. Some of you will find it much easier than others to move into this level of engagement. You may already do this naturally. Others may find it a little intimidating. Fear not. You can do it easily, because when it comes to a matter of accountability, your coaching is only related to one of two things—skills or behaviors.

The only thing required of you here is your continued effort to empower others through your own personal commitment and applied discipline, critical thinking, and problem-solving. If you choose to use these very same skills only toward achieving the business result, you've missed the opportunity to apply them toward the growth and development of another person. Remember, your employee's growth is the problem to be solved. Your employee's skill development is the business challenge to be thought through. Your employee's behavior change or skill mastery is what is to be supported.

Coaching Is an Activity, Not Just a Conversation

The mastery of coaching lies in *doing*. Your action determines the *where*, *when*, and *how* essential to producing the best possible development advantage. When you experience great coaching, it's because you perceive that coach to have a great deal of knowledge and power to compel change. Being a great manager who can effectively coach is really just about knowing what you know and having some critical tools to leverage, teach, and observe within the context of that knowledge. I'm sure any trained and certified coach who just read that sentence might be screaming, "What? It's *so* much more than that! An excellent coach is a master craftsperson in communication, teaching, and artistic leadership!" Well, if you're a professional coach, it is, yes. If you're a manager who must coach, then no, it isn't. You *can* attempt and be successful at coaching.

An opportunity to coach requires a transition in muscle use—same muscle group, different activity. You're essentially moving from sitting to standing. That's all. When you move into coaching, you change the dynamic from a conversation (specific feedback) to an applied practice (devising ways and trying out how it might be done differently and better). For example, in your coaching role, you may break down into steps a skill that you understand and do automatically, then devise a way to practice those steps via role-play in order to clarify, practice, and build confidence around a change. What was feedback and ownership for poor performance is now ownership and engagement in the next steps for improvement.

> When you move into coaching, you change the dynamic from a conversation (specific feedback) to an applied practice (devising ways and trying out how it might be done differently and better).

You'll have to assess the developmental constraints in order to start fast and go deep on the right things for the best results for the person you are coaching. Effective coaching targets higher long-term productivity, greater employee/learner satisfaction, and enhanced personal satisfaction while also driving the achievement of business objectives. When you're coaching the other person, you're still practicing being in the moment, but you're also thinking about long-term impact.

Shifting from Managing to Coaching

Let's review the difference between managing performance and coaching for development (see figure 30):

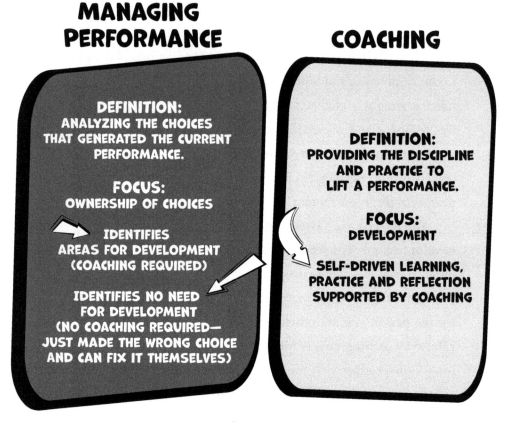

Figure 30

- Managing performance is directed at day-to-day, on-the-job, immediate analysis of how an individual chooses to apply their skills and behaviors in delivering an output. That analysis focuses on what is working for them and what is not working.

- Managing an employee's performance is centered on ownership.

A proactive manager continuously invites the other person to take ownership for their choices in applying skills and behaviors. When an employee chooses incorrectly and uses an inappropriate behavior, or when they are simply lacking the appropriate skills, managing performance involves the process of identifying where improvement is required. The conversation in which that determination is made is what has been illustrated in the Six Ownership Steps, the S.O.S. Conversation.

- Once you've identified the area of improvement, you'll begin a different relationship with your employee; the relationship will transform from *manager and employee* to *coach and learner*.

- Managing performance is centered on meeting expectations. Coaching is centered on development. Managing performance is focused on immediate time-performance issues; coaching is focused on longer-term development. Coaching is an investment in the overall growth of your employees.

CHAPTER 15

Types of Coaching

ONCE YOU CHOOSE to engage in coaching, there are two types from which to choose: day-to-day and structured coaching (see figure 31).

Day-to-day coaching is linked to managing day-to-day performance. As your employee performs their role, you may identify areas for improvement. At that point, you may immediately begin coaching the other person by having them begin practicing the corrected or improved skill or behavior. In this situation, both managing performance and coaching take place in the same meeting.

Structured coaching generally follows from a more formal appraisal like a performance assessment or performance review, or when an employee changes jobs, is seconded to another role, or undertakes an unfamiliar project—especially if it's a "stretch project" for someone you are targeting for promotion. Both of you may have identified areas for improvement, and both of you will have agreed to commit to improve the performance. You commit to coaching your employee, and your employee commits to take the learning seriously. Coaching sessions are established at regular intervals, learning assignments are given, and coaching sessions involve some kind of actual practice.

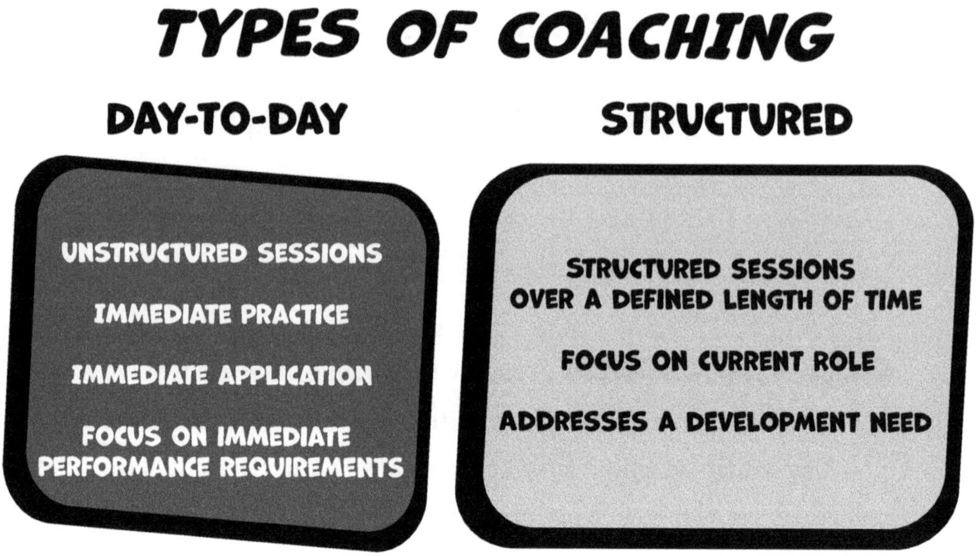

TYPES OF COACHING

DAY-TO-DAY

STRUCTURED

UNSTRUCTURED SESSIONS

IMMEDIATE PRACTICE

IMMEDIATE APPLICATION

FOCUS ON IMMEDIATE
PERFORMANCE REQUIREMENTS

STRUCTURED SESSIONS
OVER A DEFINED LENGTH OF TIME

FOCUS ON CURRENT ROLE

ADDRESSES A DEVELOPMENT NEED

Figure 31

Skills Coaching

If the outcome of your S.O.S. Conversation results in ownership of a skill deficit, then your coaching will focus on skill development (see figure 32) . This means your employee had the right motivation and the best intentions to deliver on the expectation but is struggling either because they lack a skill or need to significantly improve on one or more. These might be skills like formal training on a piece of software or gaining experience in response to a situation where they did not know what they did not know. Providing skills is akin to mentoring insofar as the person will need exposure to you or someone else with experience to give them scenario-based practice, so that they can become familiar both with what can happen and what should be done in those circumstances. Skills can also be communication skills, like effectively setting an expectation with their team or peers, holding others accountable, or effectively addressing conflict and/

or relationship building. These are all overlooked skill sets that can radically inhibit performance. How many times have you noticed your employees wrestling with questions like, "How do I handle it when someone gives me excuses or pushes back on what's expected?" or "What do I do when we don't agree on the priority for this project?"

PERFORMANCE DRIVERS & CHOICE POINTS™

WHAT ARE YOU COACHING?

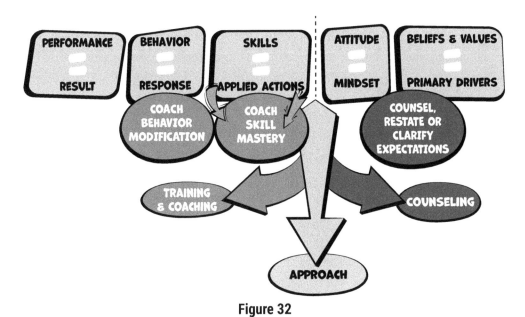

Figure 32

Likely, you have a ton of real-world experience in which you yourself have been able to make things work out well. Your best course of action as a manager is to stop, reflect, and think about how you might facilitate learning. Then, instead of offering up a laundry list of "have you tried" questions, begin with curiosity about what they have tried. Start with curiosity: "Walk me through your thinking and approach on how you are currently handling <fill in the blank>." Do not judge. Just listen. Can you locate the gap in their approach? Where is the potential error in how they are thinking about the issue? Ask a clarifying question: "Instead of doing what you're doing, what else do you think might work better or give you a different result?" If you get the deer-in-headlights look or a straight-up "I have no idea" or "I just don't know. I'm stuck," that's when you can share how you would address it. But don't stop there. The very next sentence should be: "Okay, then. Let's try it. Let's practice it now, so you get a sense of how it might go and gain some confidence to go out and try it this way." Remember, intellectually understanding how to do something differently is not the same as actually doing it differently. Your coaching must include both the understanding and the development of muscle memory that comes with practice. Take ten minutes to practice and give feedback on that practice. The intent here is to kick open the door, to familiarize, and to build skill and confidence quickly.

> Your coaching must include both the understanding and the development of muscle memory that comes with practice.

Based on the nature of the skill deficit and the ability of your employee, you can determine whether an informal session right there, as part of your S.O.S. Conversation, is appropriate or whether a more structured approach is needed.

Let's focus for a moment on coaching soft skills like communication, relationship building, or leadership. Effective coaching for these sorts of skills is based largely on improvisation—applied practice on the fly—in order to set the example, to bear witness to the skills in action, and to *be* what you are coaching your employee to *be*. There are three components here, as listed below.

Define the Skill

Give your employee an understanding of what the skill is and how it is applied. Think through how you yourself actually *do* it. Walk through that step by step, making no assumptions about what your employee knows or doesn't know already.

Illustrate the Skill

Verbalize the skill in action. *Act it out.* Let them see what you mean. Demonstrate the use of the skill. Each skill will demand a different kind of presentation. There is no formula for your performance, hence the *improvisation* part.

Construct Practice Scenarios

Engage your employee in the demonstration. As an active participant, you engage the skill, and then you allow your employee to engage in skill application while you coach them through it.

Modifying a Behavior

If the outcome of your S.O.S. Conversation results in ownership of a behavioral struggle, then your coaching is about behavior modification (see figure 33) . Your employee has previously demonstrated the skills, so you know they are capable of meeting your expectations. However, they're struggling to apply those skills consistently and as needed. Behavior issues are generally self-destructive behaviors that impede a person's ability to perform at the top of their game.

PERFORMANCE DRIVERS & CHOICE POINTS™

WHAT ARE YOU COACHING?

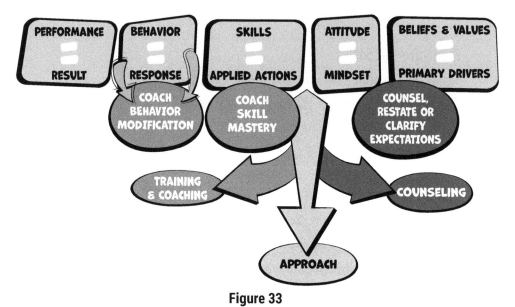

Figure 33

Let's focus here on self-defeating behaviors (SDBs). These are generally deep-seated behaviors that work against the individual and that they need to modify. *Everyone has SDBs.* Some common examples are procrastination, perfectionism, and the need to have control over others (a.k.a. overcontrolling). A sample list is set out in figure 34.

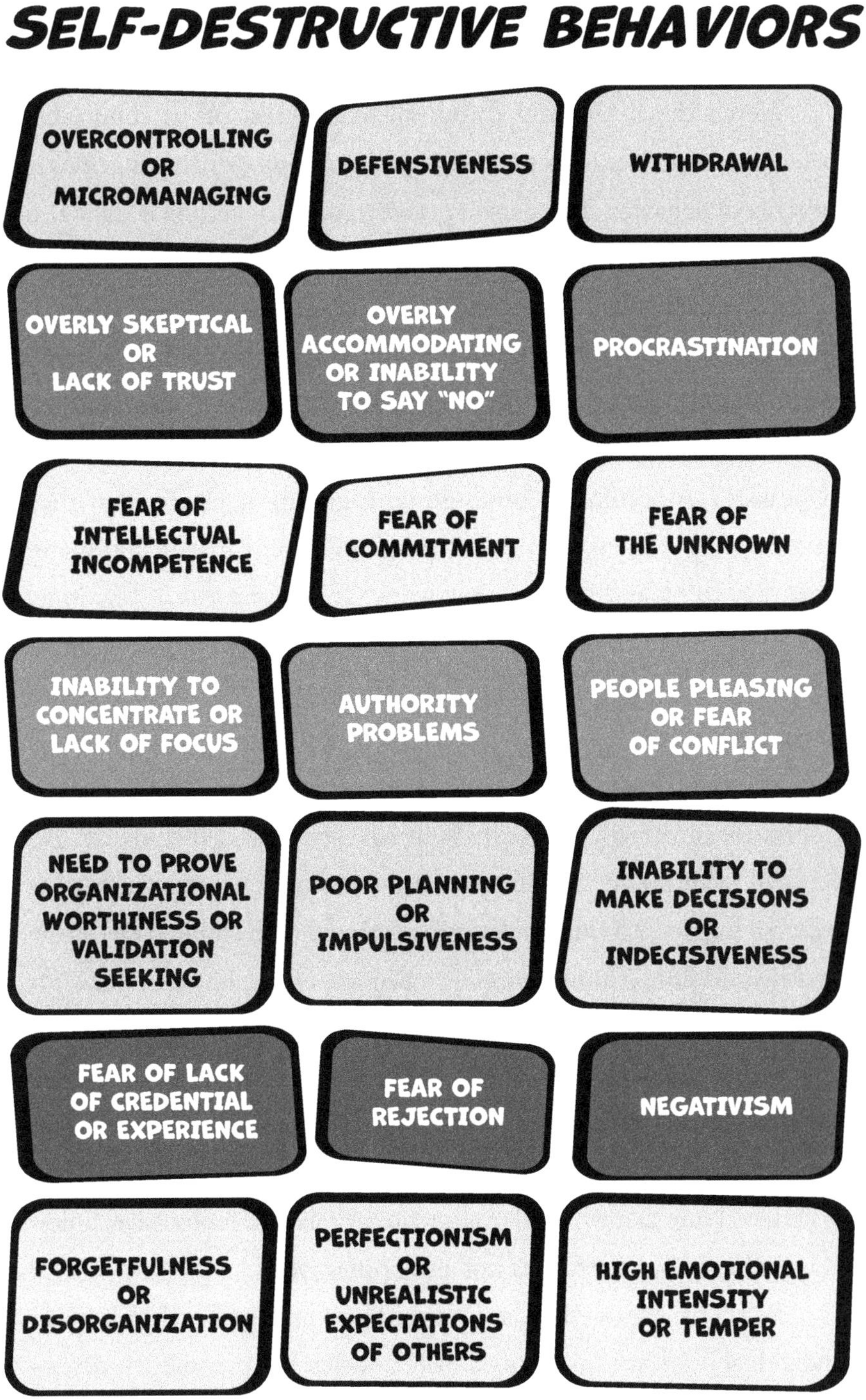

SELF-DESTRUCTIVE BEHAVIORS

OVERCONTROLLING OR MICROMANAGING	DEFENSIVENESS	WITHDRAWAL
OVERLY SKEPTICAL OR LACK OF TRUST	OVERLY ACCOMMODATING OR INABILITY TO SAY "NO"	PROCRASTINATION
FEAR OF INTELLECTUAL INCOMPETENCE	FEAR OF COMMITMENT	FEAR OF THE UNKNOWN
INABILITY TO CONCENTRATE OR LACK OF FOCUS	AUTHORITY PROBLEMS	PEOPLE PLEASING OR FEAR OF CONFLICT
NEED TO PROVE ORGANIZATIONAL WORTHINESS OR VALIDATION SEEKING	POOR PLANNING OR IMPULSIVENESS	INABILITY TO MAKE DECISIONS OR INDECISIVENESS
FEAR OF LACK OF CREDENTIAL OR EXPERIENCE	FEAR OF REJECTION	NEGATIVISM
FORGETFULNESS OR DISORGANIZATION	PERFECTIONISM OR UNREALISTIC EXPECTATIONS OF OTHERS	HIGH EMOTIONAL INTENSITY OR TEMPER

Figure 34

No doubt you will recognize SDBs that you engage in, as well as some that your colleagues, managers, friends, and family demonstrate.

Here's the interesting thing: all SDBs start off as functional behaviors. A perfectionist begins by *getting it right*, which is a perfectly functional behavior. This person gets rewarded for getting it right and in response may gradually begin to take the behavior to an extreme, becoming more obsessive in the desire not just to get it right but to get it perfect. This intensification can be brought on by higher-stakes work or a higher-profile role they've been promoted into and can then be bolstered by a need to perform well in those circumstances. A person can become so obsessed with getting it perfect that they become preoccupied with doing so to the extent that it dominates how they think and the way they work. This is one way a functional behavior becomes dysfunctional. The greater an obsession with being perfect, and the longer a person has been doing it, the more likely it's become extreme.

With SDBs, the extreme is either obsessive (internally focused) or oppressive (externally focused). Both have external consequences. An internal focus results in an internal drive and personal agenda that has external impact. An external focus is always felt and endured by others, and there is little self-awareness or reflection on the impacts. Take, for example, a perfectionist manager. She will inevitably have expectations that her team members also attain perfection in their work. This expectation will manifest itself in continually telling team members the "right way" to do everything and then reworking everything they do to make it perfect. Note that while all dysfunctional behavior is obsessive, unless it is projected on others, it is not also oppressive.

Behavior is learned. It is not hereditary or genetic. Therefore, an individual can learn to modify a behavior that has become self-defeating. At any point in time, that individual has the choice to initiate new behaviors. Once you understand that all self-defeating behaviors start out as functional, you will understand that to make the behavior functional again, you only need to *modify* it, not eliminate it. The perfectionist needs to modify their behavior back to "getting it right."

Let me say here that *not every behavioral issue is a self-destructive behavior that is extreme*. Sometimes, the issue can be a behavior that only needs to be made visible to your employee. Simply naming the behavior that's out of whack can result in snapping back to functionality. Occasionally, you'll run into an employee who's been exhibiting for a while a behavior in need of correction. These might be the employees you either inherit or that get moved around the organization like so many bags at an airport.

Before attempting to modify an SDB, you need to satisfy yourself that:

- The behavior is self-defeating.

- The behavior is able to be modified.

How to Tell if a Behavior Is Self-Defeating

A behavior would be classified as self-defeating if:

- You recognize the behavior as self-defeating and the employee recognizes the behavior as self-defeating, meaning the other person clearly knows the behavior works against them.

- Knowing it works against them, the other person chooses to engage the behavior anyway.

- They also *regularly* engage in the behavior.

Because we all have SDBs, you're bound to come across them as part of poor-performing or underperforming folks on your teams. You may also find that more performance issues and limitations are behavior-based rather than skill-based. Effectively modifying the behavior begins, of course, with ownership. Your employee must accept that the behavior is self-defeating and want to modify it—to take ownership and responsibility for making a change. This means they:

- Must be willing to assume full responsibility for their current enactment of the SDB.

- Accept that they have 100 percent ownership for the quality and direction of their life (both work and personal because SDBs affect both) and need to modify their SDB.

How to Tell if an SDB Is Modifiable

The question you'll need to answer carefully is "How dysfunctional is the SDB?" This can be answered by exploring:

- The duration of the SDB—how long they've been doing it. If it has only manifested itself in the last few years, it will be far more modifiable than an SDB that has existed for most of their lives.

- The extent of their emotional investment in the SDB. When they enact the behavior and when they talk about it, how strongly do they feel about it?

Most workplace SDBs are modifiable. However, if upon exploring the duration and emotion around an SDB you sense that it is not modifiable, then you may need to seek more professional counseling assistance.

The Counseling Conversation

If the outcome of your S.O.S. Conversation results in ownership of an attitude struggle or a conflict around beliefs and values (they don't value what you and the team value, or they're holding on to beliefs that no longer apply or are no longer true for you, the team, or even the organization), then you're going to engage in a counseling conversation (see figure 35). This means, more often than not, that the other person's choices are more emotionally driven than anything else. That means it's important to engage your emotional intelligence skills in this conversation. Be aware of the feelings they are feeling, as well as your own, and respond with empathy and curiosity to ensure trust, openness, and a way forward.

Figure 35

The strategy when addressing an attitude is to listen to the language your employee uses. Do they feel that something is "unfair" or "not right"? Realize and understand that whatever feeling they express is occurring because they are struggling with something they care about. The struggle will often reflect their desire for something to be different than it is. Maybe it's: "I should have been promoted," or "It's not fair that …" or "I don't agree with how this was set up. It's wrong." Your goal here is to maintain your empathy, to demonstrate you've heard both what they've said and how they're feeling about it, and at the same time to recognize that agreements and decisions have been made, the role is what the role is, and the established expectations are, more than likely, not going to change. What *can* change is how this person is both thinking about and approaching the issue and the choice(s) they are currently making. They have full control there. What would they like to do? This can sometimes come down to a heartfelt conversation about fit. Is this person still a fit for the team, the role, the organization? That's a real question. When you ask, it should never be threatening; instead, it should be about self-reflection. Can you work with them to find a better fit?

Here's an example:

Manager	Hi, Tanya. Thanks for coming in. I wanted to talk to you about a behavior pattern I'm seeing, which impacts the team in a negative way. I feel it's something you can address easily. The expectation is that everyone on the team is here and ready to work at 8:00 a.m. I'm concerned because you consistently choose to show up between thirty and forty-five minutes late on a regular basis. Everyone else on your team shows up on time. Because there is a pattern here, this is now creating conflict on your team, and I want to address it now before it gets worse. Can you talk to me about this?	Set the table. Share your issue.
Tanya	I understand what you're telling me. I'm sorry that they see it as problematic. However, I do get my work done, and they know that. I don't think I'm letting anybody down; am I? There's a lot of time spent just standing around and gabbing at the beginning of the day, and nobody's really getting started first thing. So I think my timing is good as I get right to work when I get in.	Denial of ownership
Manager	Yes. I see how you see it. The issue is about maintaining a team standard. The standard is there in service of both the team and the client that your team serves. It sounds to me like you may not value that standard and how it impacts your team relationships.	Address the attitude.

| Tanya | *It's not that I don't value the team relationships. I do. I just don't think it's that big of a deal or that it's really having that much of an impact, especially when I'm doing my part on the team.* | Denial of ownership |
| Manager | *That's just it, though. Doing your part on the team includes being here on time. That's the expectation for all of you. That's the expectation of the client as well. Is being here on time, at 8:00 a.m. each day, something you're willing to take responsibility for? If not, and this is something you really want to hold your ground on, that's fine. But it means that you won't continue to be a good fit on this team. If you're unwilling to abide by the standards the team has set, are you willing to explore other teams in the organization who may not have issues around an 8:00 a.m. start?* | Define the long-term implications of choice. Remember to approach with a supportive tone and curiosity, but be definitive about the expectations. |

When you're counseling choices that center around beliefs, values, and attitudes, the strategy will more often be focused on addressing an internal conflict your employee may be having about what's true and important. For example: "It's clear you're in conflict about how we're prioritizing the project. If that's really where it is for you, the question is: How long do you want to allow this to get in the way of your participation?" Conflict resolution is always a question of time because a person must actively work to let it go, and that can take a while. For some, that can take much longer than is tolerable or healthy for the team or the business. If left unresolved, these can become questions of dismissal. Changing a person's beliefs takes a lot of new truth, and we've already discussed the ways that your responsibilities as a manager needn't involve changing anyone else's truths. In a moment like this, you either work to engage a resolution strategy the other person designs, owns, and actively participates in for a specific period of time (and that works for both the person and the company— Personal Improvement Plans, a.k.a. PIPs), or you acknowledge the beginning of the end of the working relationship.

Tips to Excel In Your Coaching

If you're approaching coaching as a manager, keep in mind the following points:

- **Good coaching is a willing partnership**. Your buy-in and readiness to assist your employee is as important as their willingness to take ownership for the issue they took responsibility for in your S.O.S. Conversation and for their own development. Willingness is about commitment of time and energy toward development. When you're willing, you'll relay your confidence in and passion about your ability to successfully develop the performance of another person. You'll demonstrate desire and conviction about the value you bring to coaching up your team. If you're really not interested in supporting development, why would your employees be interested? As a manager, you are always modeling the way things are done.

- **Seek mutual satisfaction**. At the end of each coaching session, you and your employee should experience a true sense of personal satisfaction—you for instilling the most productive practices and the employee for progressively gaining more experience and comfort applying the skill nearer to the desired level. When you or your employee leaves a session dissatisfied with the effort, no satisfaction is experienced. Satisfaction is the measuring stick of success or failure on the learning or development curve.

- **How you communicate sets the tone and determines success**. Through your open and encouraging communication, your employee is stretched to achieve their potential. You provide the vision and the direction, and you fix the achievable goal in the employee's imagination. You draw the scene and set the stage for the learner's performance with your voice, your inflection, and your well-thought-out and well-articulated words. You provide fair and rational feedback. You analyze your employee's practiced performance, always illustrating, teaching, or guiding with the sole purpose of ensuring that your employee's desire to achieve is kept intact, so the skill can be successfully acquired and utilized. This is essential trust-building that shifts the working relationship you already have to a higher level. When you effectively bring your coaching abilities into play, your employees no longer doubt your intentions nor question your desire for their best performance.

- **Observe and pay close attention**. Read the room as you're coaching. Watch and pay attention in the moment to your employee and the environment. Watch for both verbal and nonverbal cues, visible affects (mannerisms that distract), and "tells" (those nonverbal indicators that communicate a message). It's not just what's said but all the things that go into how they say it.

- **In order to appropriately pace the learning and practice, be aware of your employee's concerns and their degree of challenge or discomfort**. Keep an eye out for signals that your employee is disengaging from the learning and practice; these signs might include being preoccupied, unprepared, or continually late to coaching sessions. Address these as soon as you recognize them.

- **Work on real stuff.** Out of discomfort and to take the pressure off a little, you might be tempted to make up situations that allow your employee to feel safer in a practice environment. It's always easier and more effective when you discuss and analyze actual challenges or relevant work performance issues when you're practicing new skills. This keeps the conversation true and open while working to address and improve real results. Practicing targeted what-ifs is okay, but practicing something concocted in an alternate universe limits the growth and stymies the potential impact of the practice.

- **Role-play is the fastest and the most potent tool for coaching**. In all coaching, scenario-based role-play is the quintessential key to unlocking the potential of your employee and constructively guiding them to grow and improve their skills. Your goal as a coach is to be competent in creating, driving, and participating in scenarios. With improvisation, you avoid rote repetition and meet head-on the challenges of the unknown.

- **Look to your employee for scenarios.** Let them build the roles based on their own experiences. Through the spontaneous creation of the scenario, your employee will begin to actively understand how to identify opportunities in which to apply a new skill. You provide the guardrails and ensure the scenarios are appropriate to the skill and don't wander off track. Improvisation is not scary. Everyone can improvise. As people, we learn through experience and experiencing. When the environment is engaging, anyone can learn whatever they choose to learn. When coaching, it is your responsibility to create and maintain a learning environment that is compelling, nurturing, and supportive in order to engage your employee on all the learning levels: intellectual (the scenario), physical (working face-to-face), and intuitive (the freedom to try and change how they apply what they are learning). Of those three levels of learning, the intuitive is the most vital. It's what cements choices and builds confidence. Skills are developed at the very moment the learner is having all the fun role-playing has to offer—this is the exact time they are open to receiving them.

- **Role-playing is psychologically different in degree but not in kind to everyday interactions.** The ability to create a situation imaginatively and to play a role in it involves a kind of psychological freedom, the freedom to create the condition in which strain and conflict are dissolved and potentialities are released in a spontaneous effort to meet the demands of the situation and the learning challenge.

- **Any scenario worth playing is highly social and personal and has within it a problem that requires solving—an objective point at which each individual must become involved.** As you role-play, you grow more alert, ready, and eager for anything unusual as you respond to happenings simultaneously. Your personal capacity to involve yourself in the problem of the scenario and to engage the multiple stimuli the scenario provokes is what determines the extent of your growth.

The final word is this: the more those you coach role-play their way into trying new approaches, improving skills, attempting conversational outcomes, and building relationships, the better they will become at standing in all the moments they face. You think on your feet, learn, and improve through role-play. That's a skill that will serve you throughout your career, whether you manage others or not.

CHAPTER 16

Owning Up

OWNING UP TO YOUR CHOICES and decisions is the heart of accountability. Every day you make a myriad of decisions about how you spend your time, about the quality of your work, about what's important, and about when you're done—and that's to name just a few. All of your choices have impacts on the results you generate. In this sense, you are no different than anyone you manage or lead.

Ownership is an act of personal power. It's an act that says, "I am in control of my decisions, and I am willing to accept the impact of my decisions regardless of how things go." Ownership demands self-confidence, and it demands self-reflection—not self-protection. In an age of *fake* everything (thank you, internet), our ability to be real with each other is paramount to our success as people, as well as in business. We are all tired of being lied to, politicked, and diverted by meaningless finger-pointing and scapegoating. It's exhausting and time-consuming, and it costs everyone money, trust, and well-being. The absence of accountability takes the joy out of work. If we're not able to succeed in the efforts we make on a daily basis, we can quickly become disheartened.

Happiness comes from the ability to solve the problem. If your problem is holding others accountable, now is the time to find your joy.

Bringing others to a place of ownership is a simple process brought to fruition through a higher capability around specific communication and critical-thinking skills.

The process is simple and straightforward. However, it requires focus and practice to achieve the desired effect.

Owning Up in 360 Degrees

If you're going to achieve accountability as an organization, accountability is everybody's job. It's a skill set that should be leveraged in every direction, meaning it starts with you. You use it in your down-line relationships with your direct reports, you use it in your peer and teammate relationships, and you use it in your up-line relationship with your boss or team leads. When you can do this as a matter of course in your work (and maybe even at home), that is when you truly have mastery. Here's an example of what a good version of the S.O.S. Conversation looks and sounds like at work. We are picking up the conversation at Steps 5 and 6 after all the reflection and thinking work of Steps 1 through 4 has

> If you're going to achieve accountability as an organization, accountability is everybody's job.

been done. Notice the subtle changes in language based on who is seeking accountability and initiating the conversation.

Manager-Employee Conversation

Manager: Hi, Xavier. Thank you for coming in. I wanted to speak to you about your performance with the Wowza account, in that you've got an opportunity to raise your game here. My expectation was that you'd have delivered three solid ideas to the team by last week to get the project moving forward. I'm concerned because you've still yet to produce those or share them with your team. The impact to both the team and ultimately the client is two-fold. Your team's trust in you is diminished, and the client's trust in us organizationally is now at risk. Can you talk to me about that?

Listen—Accept or Reject?

Xavier: Yes, I know I'm running behind. I'm massively overcommitted between this project and the one I'm on with Sarah's team. I'm working on everything. I'm just having a hard time managing the deadlines for so many. I'll have something to the team this week.

Clarify Ownership

Manager: It sounds to me like you understand your responsibility and take ownership for your late delivery. Is that correct?

Xavier: Yes. Absolutely!

Develop

Manager: I heard a lot of reasons why this is happening for you. Let me just ask you a couple questions. When you knew you were going to be late on this project, what did you choose to do?

Xavier: I don't know. I'm not sure what you mean.

Manager: Take a moment and think back to last week or the week prior, whenever it was you realized that you were not going to submit the ideas to your team by the deadline. In that moment when you knew you weren't going to make it, what did you choose to do?

Listen For Choice Point

Xavier: Well, I probably thought, *They're just going to have to wait. I've got too many competing priorities.* So I prioritized Sarah's team's work because it was easier. I thought I could get it off my plate then return to this project with a clear head to get something that had the right quality.

Check For Skill Or Behavior

Manager: I see. Okay. So you made a judgment call on how to prioritize your work. What else could you have done in that moment that would have generated a better outcome for everyone?

Xavier: Well, obviously, for starters I should have let everyone know how I was prioritizing to manage expectations better.

[Pause. Leverage Silence]

Xavier: And I probably should have consulted both you and Sarah to double-check my thinking, as I know now that Sarah's client has more time built in to the deadline. I was just focused on how I saw it.

What's the Behavior Change Needed?

Manager: I agree. I'm glad to hear that you are aware of how your decisions created the result we're now managing. In moving forward, what do you think would help you in the future to apply this learning when it comes to this kind of dilemma in your work?

Xavier: That's a great question. I think this conversation will probably come back to mind. But I think perhaps I need to think about the teams more.

Manager: I agree. Your results are not your own. These are team results. That requires a higher degree of collaboration all the way around. While you've got autonomy over the work you deliver to the team, deadline decisions are team decisions.

Xavier: Yes. Maybe the best thing I can do is bring this to the team so we can all decide the protocol together. I'm sure this will come up for me again, and I'd like to know how they want me to handle it.

Manager: Great idea. Let's put it on the agenda for Tuesday.

Peer-to-Peer Conversation

Maeve: Hi, Xavier. Thank you for stopping in. I wanted to speak to you about how we're working together on the Wowza account, in that we need to raise our game here. I was expecting that you'd have delivered at least three solid ideas to the team by last week to get this project moving forward. I'm concerned because you've still yet to produce those or share them with us. This is creating a couple issues. I feel like my ability to rely on you is at risk, and the client's trust in us organizationally has come up. Can you talk to me about that?

Listen—Accept or Reject?

Xavier: Yes, I know I'm running behind. I'm sorry. I'm massively over-committed between this project and the one I'm on with Sarah's team. I'm working on everything. I'm just having a hard time managing the deadlines for so many. I'll have something to you guys this week.

Clarify Ownership

Maeve: I understand. We all have competing commitments. That said, how can we rely on you when it's not clear how you are prioritizing?

Xavier: I see what you mean. I didn't let anyone know what I was doing and what to expect. I've just been feeling overwhelmed and thought it best to press on as best I could. What would you suggest I do?

Develop

Maeve: Well, I'm certain it's not just me. Let's bring this to the team, so we can all decide on how we should deal with communication on competing deadlines and priorities. I just want to be sure we're all clear, because when one of us doesn't deliver, then the whole team can't deliver. How about I put out a notice to the team for a brief meeting on this tomorrow?

Xavier: That would be great. Thanks for letting me know how you feel. I appreciate your candor. I'd like to be thought of as reliable. Let's figure this out together. Thanks!

Employee-Manager Conversation

Xavier: Hi, Boss! Thank you for making time to meet with me. I wanted to talk to you about your commitment on the Wowza account to provide additional resources for the project. My expectation, and I think the team's expectation, was that you were going to provide us with an additional person for at least the first part of the project to ensure we delivered on milestones. I'm concerned because I'm up against it getting solid ideas to the team, as I've got competing priorities with Sarah's team's work as well. I'm concerned because we're getting to a place where my credibility is going to be at risk, not to mention the client impact. Can you tell me where things are?

Listen—Accept or Reject?

Boss: Yes, I know I'm running behind. I've reached out to secure Tabitha but have not heard back from her manager to see if I can utilize her for the next few months.

Clarify Ownership

Xavier: Great. It sounds to me like you are hearing my urgency. Is there something in my thinking that needs to change? Or do you feel like you'll be able to get Tabitha on board by next week?

Boss: Yes. I hear your urgency. Leave it with me. I will get with Tabitha's manager this afternoon and sort this out by the end of the week. If I can't get Tabitha, I will let the team know what to expect as an alternative. Thanks, Xavier. I appreciate you giving me the nudge.

Xavier: You bet. Thanks for your time. I'm looking forward to an additional teammate.

Final Review

Every skill and ability I discuss in this book is within your grasp. There is nothing here that you can't do. You can start today; heck, you can start right now. You can master everything in this book in a very short period of time. Let's have a quick review of the big picture and focus on the fact that there are only Six Ownership Steps to take.

In a nutshell, here's what I'm asking you to practice:

1. **Identify *your* issue.** Accountability starts with you. Drill down; think past the results to the issue at hand.

2. **Analyze the choice point** for the disappointing result (see the **Performance Drivers & Choice Points** diagram). *Why* do you have this result? At what point does it seem that the other person made a poor choice?

3. **Explore the impacts.** What are the impacts of this choice beyond just the bad result? Think both in terms of how it impacts you and also how it impacts the business, team, and associated people, systems, and processes, and the person whose choice it was.

4. **Rehearse yourself!** Practice out loud the conversation you want to have. What exactly is the feedback you are going to give? How will you start that conversation? How will you know if you've gotten ownership? What are the likely responses you'll get? How will you handle a plausible variety of responses this person might give you?

ACCOUNTABILITY S.O.S.™ PRACTICE

Figure 36

5. **Have the conversation.** Keep in mind this is the fifth of six steps. If you have not engaged the first four, your chances of successfully achieving ownership and change are extremely low.

6. **Facilitate solutions around ownership.** Do not tell people what they *need* to do. Guide solution building through discovery and open questions, drive critical thinking, and learn what they know and what they don't by discovering how they think.

Here are some tips for your continued success:

- *Listen!* Listening is 50 percent of your conversation. It's how you establish conversational guardrails that steer toward a successful outcome.

- ***Deal with denial or rejection of ownership.*** Don't *eat the plastic fruit.*

- ***Always administer consequences when no ownership is taken.*** Do not change role expectations or let a lack of ownership lie. There is no accountability without consequence for its absence.

- *Take what you can get.* If all you can get is partial ownership, start with that. Get the rest later. Accountability is not a competition or winner-take-all approach. Build on small wins.

- *Facilitate change.* Don't forget what full accountability looks like. Full accountability is not just about owning up to the bad choice but also about owning up to the choice to do better, clarity about what better looks like, and the activity of improvement.

Your ability to achieve full accountability as a manager can involve guiding your employees toward self-improvement through coaching and development support of their behavior shifts, their skill development, and their overall professional growth. Every bad result and every bad decision is an opportunity for learning. We are humbled by failure, and it's humility that unlocks the door to learning—*so long as we are supported and encouraged and can find courage in our vulnerability*. Humility shuts the door on learning when we are criticized and made to feel shamed and blamed in our vulnerability. The ultimate choice you make as a manager is how to turn others' vulnerability into courage and opportunity to help them grow.

What Now?

If this book spoke to you and you'd like to learn more, here are some things you can do to move forward:

Go to own-up.com and download the *resources* I have provided for you there. You'll find a worksheet for mapping out your conversations. Use the worksheet as you prepare to practice the conversation out loud and in advance of engaging the other person. You'll find a printable S.O.S. Conversation diagram to aid your ongoing efforts and to help you visualize what you need to do. Put the diagram somewhere you'll see it regularly. You'll find a guide for taking the 120-day Accountability Challenge. That's right, you should be able to transform your practice and your work environment in four months! You'll also find links to the OwnUp! podcasts to help you integrate your reading into your work.

Get a coach or take a course. Individuals and groups can sign up for coaching sessions at own-up.com. A coaching package, live webinar, or online course will help you master these skills in a few short weeks.

To receive a discount on any or all of these, go to www.own-up.com where you can upload your proof of purchase for this book, and we'll hook you up! And yes, if for some reason you bought more than one, you'll get a better discount! Thanks in advance for that. Focusing your practice on actual issues with the help of a knowledgeable guide is the absolute quickest way to gain competence and confidence. All courses include coaching sessions to help you apply your learnings in real time on issues that are significant for you.

If you haven't already, try running through the Six Steps. Practice in real time on a real issue. Use the S.O.S. Conversation for holding someone accountable. It's why you picked up this book. This is your choice point.

ACKNOWLEDGMENTS

This book has been a work in progress for decades. It has been through many years of proving out the content. It has also been in a draft form more than once. I would like to acknowledge both the time and patience it's taken to get here. It's also taken an army of people who have supported both this work and me personally to bring it across the finish line.

First, I'd like to acknowledge my team, which is also my family. Beginning with my brother Chip who has worked with me through thick and thin to build a business against, at times, what seemed like insurmountable odds. We've been thick as thieves since we were small, and if there's anybody who can add amazing ideas, be brutally honest, entertain crazy thoughts, have fun, and build a doable process to get shit done, it's Chip.

Next, I'd like to acknowledge my husband, Steve, who has been the best life partner both for his unending support of me as a person but also as an entrepreneur and a business professional. My copious travel schedule compares only to the amount of patience and love he's given me to build myself and my business at the same time we built an amazing family.

I want to be sure to acknowledge my kids as well, because without my boys Connor and Jack, I would not have been able to test out and improve my skills with as much of my work practice at home. Emotional intelligence and accountability have been run through its paces at our house. I'm particularly proud of how they've turned out.

I want to acknowledge my coaching team, Richard Rodriguez and Peter Lyddon, who are really responsible for pushing me the last miles to the finish in this work. They have been a great source of support and positivity because I never knew how much self-doubt you really have to endure to get a book written. They never thought twice and kept badgering in the most supportive way!

A special and heartfelt acknowledgment for Brian Quinette who has been there with me in creativity, in life, in work, and on game nights when it mattered most.

I also want to acknowledge the friends, clients, and clients who've become friends, who have been on the receiving end of my work or who've had to listen to me talk endlessly about my work over a cocktail, or three, on a barstool or in a beach chair. These include some folks who actively supported my work on this book. Thanks to Bill Flowers, Jill Farschman, Peggy Hermann, and Lori Piddick. I'd also like to include my cheerleaders, chums, and a particular member of the Pony Squad—you know who you are.

There are also some steady client relationships that must be acknowledged in that these people allowed me to work continuously with them and their teams, which allowed me to be better in the time we worked and continue to work together.

I want to acknowledge my friend and colleague Angie Lee and all the work she's done with me creatively over the years. She's really helped the book come to life as she's done with so many other projects in life, theater, and work. A shout-out to my new BFF and editor Jennifer Holt who has been fantastic helping to keep it clear. Clear is kind!

Lastly, I'd like to acknowledge the support of Peter Miller, Paul Atkinson, Russell Perriera, and Jason Kates in Sydney, Australia, and all the coaches who helped service clients over the years of the business where we've never stopped asking: "So what part of that are you willing to own?"

.

CPSIA information can be obtained
at www.ICGtesting.com
Printed in the USA
BVHW041635240222
630017BV00001B/2/J